First World War
and Army of Occupation
War Diary
France, Belgium and Germany

1 DIVISION
1 Infantry Brigade
Coldstream Guards
1 Battalion
13 August 1914 - 31 July 1917

WO95/1263/1

The Naval & Military Press Ltd
www.nmarchive.com
Published in association with The National Archives

Published by

The Naval & Military Press Ltd

Unit 10 Ridgewood Industrial Park,

Uckfield, East Sussex,

TN22 5QE England

Tel: +44 (0) 1825 749494

www.naval-military-press.com

www.nmarchive.com

Contents

Document type	Place/Title	Date From	Date To
Heading	WO95/1263/1		
Heading	1st Division 1st Battalion Coldstream Guards Aug-Dec 1914 1914Aug-1915 July To Guards Div		
Heading	1st Guards 1st Division. 1st Battalion Coldstream Guards August 1914		
War Diary	Farnboro	13/08/1914	14/08/1914
War Diary	Rest Camp-Le Havre	15/08/1914	15/08/1914
War Diary	Le Havre	16/08/1914	16/08/1914
War Diary	Boue	17/08/1914	21/08/1914
War Diary	Cartignes	22/08/1914	22/08/1914
War Diary	Vieux Reng	23/08/1914	23/08/1914
War Diary	Rouveroy	24/08/1914	24/08/1914
War Diary	La Longueville	25/08/1914	25/08/1914
War Diary	Dompierre	26/08/1914	31/08/1914
Heading	1st Guards brigade. 1st Division 1st Battalion Coldstream Guards September 1914		
War Diary	Fesmy	27/08/1914	27/08/1914
War Diary	Janqueuse	28/08/1914	28/08/1914
War Diary	St. Gobain	29/08/1914	30/08/1914
War Diary	Pinon	31/08/1914	31/08/1914
War Diary	Missy	01/09/1914	01/09/1914
War Diary	La Ferte-Milon	02/09/1914	02/09/1914
War Diary	Chambry	03/09/1914	03/09/1914
War Diary	Jouarre	04/09/1914	04/09/1914
War Diary	Coulommiers	05/09/1914	05/09/1914
War Diary	Nesles	06/09/1914	06/09/1914
War Diary	Puiseau	07/09/1914	07/09/1914
War Diary	Le Temple	08/09/1914	08/09/1914
War Diary	N Bassevelle	09/09/1914	09/09/1914
War Diary	N Lucy-Le-Gocage	10/09/1914	10/09/1914
War Diary	Latilly	11/09/1914	11/09/1914
War Diary	Bruyeres	12/09/1914	12/09/1914
War Diary	Bazoches	13/09/1914	13/09/1914
War Diary	Battle at the Aisne	14/09/1914	14/09/1914
War Diary	Vendresse	15/09/1914	18/09/1914
War Diary	Troyon Ridge	19/09/1914	19/09/1914
War Diary	Oeuilly	20/09/1914	21/09/1914
War Diary	Verneuil	22/09/1914	23/09/1914
War Diary	Ferme de Metz	24/09/1914	26/09/1914
War Diary	Oeuilly	27/09/1914	27/09/1914
War Diary	N. of Troyon	28/09/1914	14/10/1914
Miscellaneous Diagram etc	1st Bn. Coldstream Gds Sept 14th, 1914	29/09/1914	29/09/1914
Diagram etc	1st Bn. Coldstream Gds Sept 14th 1914		
Miscellaneous Diagram etc	680 II Grade 1st Division	29/09/1914	29/09/1914
Miscellaneous	A Form Messages And Signals		
Miscellaneous	Dear Edmonds	16/00/1900	16/00/1900
Heading	1st Guards Brigade. 1st Division 1st Battalion The Coldstream Guards October 1914		

War Diary	N. of Troyon	28/09/1914	14/10/1914
War Diary	Troyon	15/10/1914	15/10/1914
War Diary	Blanzy	16/10/1914	17/10/1914
War Diary	Hazebrouck	18/10/1914	19/10/1914
War Diary	Poperinghe	20/10/1914	21/10/1914
War Diary	Langemarck	22/10/1914	25/10/1914
War Diary	N Zillibeke Rested	26/10/1914	26/10/1914
War Diary	Gheluvelt	27/10/1914	31/10/1914
Miscellaneous	Orders	04/10/1914	04/10/1914
Miscellaneous	Report On attack on German "Fish-house" trench On The Night Of Oct 4/5th 1914	05/10/1914	05/10/1914
Miscellaneous	Vendresse Oct 5th ?/14		
Heading	1st Guards Brigade. 1st Division. 1st Battalion The Coldstream Guards November 1914		
War Diary	Gheluvelt	29/10/1914	29/10/1914
War Diary	N. Gheluvelt	30/10/1914	05/11/1914
War Diary	N. of Gheluvelt	06/11/1914	12/11/1914
War Diary	Zonnebeke	13/11/1914	16/11/1914
War Diary	N. Klein Zillibeke	17/11/1914	20/11/1914
War Diary	Meteren	21/11/1914	23/11/1914
War Diary	Strazeele	24/11/1914	30/11/1914
Heading	1st Guards Brigade. 1st Division 1st Battalion Coldstream Guards December 1914		
War Diary	Strazeele	28/11/1914	20/12/1914
War Diary	Bethune	21/12/1914	21/12/1914
War Diary	Pont Fixe	21/12/1914	21/12/1914
War Diary	Givenchy	21/12/1914	22/12/1914
War Diary	Pont Fixe	23/12/1914	23/12/1914
War Diary	Givenchy & Cambrin	23/12/1914	23/12/1914
War Diary	Cambrin	24/12/1914	25/12/1914
War Diary	Cambrin Givenchy	26/12/1914	26/12/1914
War Diary	Givenchy	27/12/1914	27/12/1914
War Diary	Givenchy and billetted at Bethune	28/12/1914	28/12/1914
War Diary	Bethune	29/12/1914	30/12/1914
War Diary	Beury	31/12/1914	31/12/1914
Miscellaneous	3rd Echelon	26/02/1915	26/02/1915
Heading	1st Division 1st Brigade 1st Battalion Coldstream Guards Jan-July 1915		
Heading	1st Division 1st Brigade War Diary 1st Coldstream Guards January 1915		
Miscellaneous	1st Coldstream Guards	01/01/1915	01/01/1915
War Diary	Annequin Givenchy	02/01/1915	02/01/1915
War Diary	Givenchy	03/01/1915	13/01/1915
War Diary	Givenchy and billetted at Bethune	13/01/1915	13/01/1915
War Diary	Bethune	14/01/1915	20/01/1915
War Diary	Bethune and billetted at Cambrian	21/01/1915	21/01/1915
War Diary	Cambrin	22/01/1915	22/01/1915
War Diary	Cambrin and trenches at Cuinchy	23/01/1915	23/01/1915
War Diary	Cuinchy	24/01/1915	25/01/1915
War Diary	Cuinchy and billetted at Bethune	26/01/1915	26/01/1915
War Diary	Bethune	27/01/1915	30/01/1915
War Diary	Bethune and billetted at Oblingham	30/01/1915	30/01/1915
War Diary	Oblingham and billeted at Ecquedecques	31/01/1915	31/01/1915
War Diary	Ecquedecques	01/02/1915	04/02/1915
Heading	War Diary 1st Coldstream Guards February 1915		
War Diary	Ecquedecques	01/02/1915	27/02/1915

War Diary	Ecquedecques and billetted at Hinges	27/02/1915	27/02/1915
War Diary	Hinges and billetted at Richebourg Lavoue	28/02/1915	28/02/1915
Heading	War Diary 1st Coldstream Guards March 1915		
War Diary	Richebourg L'Avoue	01/03/1915	04/03/1915
War Diary	Richebourg L'Avoue and billetts at Le Touret	04/03/1915	04/03/1915
War Diary	Le Touret	05/03/1915	05/03/1915
War Diary	Le Touret and trenches at Richebourg L'Avoue	06/03/1915	06/03/1915
War Diary	Richebourg L'Avoue	07/03/1915	07/03/1915
War Diary	Richebourg L'Avoue and billetts at Le Touret	08/03/1915	08/03/1915
War Diary	Le Touret	09/03/1915	10/03/1915
War Diary	Le Touret and trenches at Richebourg L'Avoue	11/03/1915	11/03/1915
War Diary	Richebourg L'Avoue	12/03/1915	14/03/1915
War Diary	Billets in Le Touret	15/03/1915	15/03/1915
War Diary	Le Touret Battn in billets	16/03/1915	16/03/1915
War Diary	Trenches S. of Rue du Bois	17/03/1915	18/03/1915
War Diary	Billets in Le Touret	19/03/1915	20/03/1915
War Diary	Trenches S of Rue du Bois	21/03/1915	22/03/1915
War Diary	Billets in Bethune	23/03/1915	24/03/1915
War Diary	Billets at Cornet Malo	25/03/1915	30/03/1915
War Diary	Trenches S of Richebourg L'Avoue	31/03/1915	03/04/1915
Heading	1st Infantry Brigade. 1st Division. War Diary 1st Coldstream Guards April 1915		
Heading	On His Majesty's Service.		
War Diary	Trenches S. of Richebourg L'Avoue	01/04/1915	03/04/1915
War Diary	Billets at Le Touret & Richebourg St Vaast	04/04/1915	07/04/1915
War Diary	Trenches S of Richebourg L'Avoue	08/04/1915	15/04/1915
War Diary	Billets at Cornet Malo	16/04/1915	17/04/1915
War Diary	Billets in Cornet Malo	18/04/1915	23/04/1915
War Diary	Billets in Cornet Malo to billets in Oblinghem	24/04/1915	24/04/1915
War Diary	Billets in Oblinghem	25/04/1915	30/04/1915
Heading	1st Infantry Brigade. 1st Division.War Diary 1st Coldstream Guards May 1915		
War Diary		01/05/1915	02/05/1915
War Diary	Billets & dug outs N. of Richebourg L'Avoue	03/05/1915	04/05/1915
War Diary	Breastworks S. of Richebourg L'Avoue	05/05/1915	08/05/1915
War Diary	Operation at Rue du Bois	09/05/1915	09/05/1915
War Diary	Billets in Hinges	10/05/1915	12/05/1915
War Diary	Billets in Le Preol	13/05/1915	13/05/1915
War Diary	Billets in Bethune	14/05/1915	15/05/1915
War Diary	Billets at Sailly La Bourse	16/05/1915	17/05/1915
War Diary	Billets in Sailly La Bourse	17/05/1915	19/05/1915
War Diary	Trenches near Le Rutoire	20/05/1915	20/05/1915
War Diary	Trenches E of Le Rutoire	21/05/1915	23/05/1915
War Diary	Billets in Sailly La Bourse	24/05/1915	27/05/1915
War Diary	Trenches East of Le Rutoire (near Vermelles)	28/05/1915	29/05/1915
War Diary	Trenches East of Le Rutoire	30/05/1915	31/05/1915
Miscellaneous	Brigade Operation Orders		
Operation(al) Order(s)	Operation Order No. 5 by Brigadier-General, H.C. Lowther, C.V.O., C.M.G., D.S.O. Commanding 1st Guards Brigade	16/05/1915	16/05/1915
Miscellaneous	The Following Notes On Necessary Work In The Trenches are Circulated to all Battalions in Order That They May Know What to Carry On With as Soon as They Take Over	16/05/1915	16/05/1915
Miscellaneous	Colds Gds	26/05/1915	26/05/1915

Heading	1st Infantry Brigade. 1st Division. War Diary 1st Coldstream Guards June 1915		
Miscellaneous	On His Majesty's Service.		
Miscellaneous	1st Coldstream Guards June 1915		
War Diary	Billets in Bethune (Tobacco Factory)	02/06/1915	10/06/1915
War Diary	Cambrin Defences	11/06/1915	13/06/1915
War Diary	Trenches nr Cuinchy A. 2	14/06/1915	14/06/1915
War Diary	Trenches at Cuinchy	15/06/1915	16/06/1915
War Diary	Billets in Montmorency Bks Bethune	17/06/1915	22/06/1915
War Diary	Billets in Bethune Montmorency BKs	23/06/1915	23/06/1915
War Diary	Moved to billets in Burbure	24/06/1917	24/06/1917
War Diary	Billets in Burbure	25/06/1915	28/06/1915
War Diary	Billets in Burbure to Vaudricourt	29/06/1915	29/06/1915
War Diary	Billets in Vaudricourt	30/06/1915	30/06/1915
Miscellaneous	Appendices		
Miscellaneous	A Form Messages And Signals		
Miscellaneous	C Form (Duplicate). Messages And Signals		
Miscellaneous	Cold Gds.	04/06/1915	04/06/1915
Miscellaneous	Cold Gds.	08/06/1915	08/06/1915
Miscellaneous	A Form. Messages And Signals.		
Miscellaneous	Coldstream Guards The Following Received From 1st Division, Begins	16/06/1915	16/06/1915
Miscellaneous	A Form. Messages And Signals		
Miscellaneous	A Form. Messages And Signals.		
Heading	1st Infantry Brigade 1st Division.War Diary 1st Coldstream Guards July 1915		
Miscellaneous	On His Majesty's Service.		
War Diary	Billets in Vaudricourt	01/07/1915	05/07/1915
War Diary	Billets in Vaudricourt to La Bourse	05/07/1915	05/07/1915
War Diary	Billets in La Bourse	05/07/1915	06/07/1915
War Diary	La Bourse	07/07/1915	09/07/1915
War Diary	Trenches at Le Rutoire	10/07/1915	13/07/1915
War Diary	Billets in Vermelles	14/07/1915	15/07/1915
War Diary	Billets in Vermelles To Trenches nr Le Rutoire	16/07/1915	16/07/1915
War Diary	Trenches E of Vermelles (Le Rutoire)	17/05/1915	19/05/1915
War Diary	Billets in Bethune	19/05/1915	25/07/1915
War Diary	Billets in Bethune to Billets in Sailly La Bourse	25/07/1915	28/07/1915
War Diary	Billets in Bethune to Trenches S of the La Bassee Bethune Road	28/07/1915	28/07/1915
War Diary	Trenches S of Bethune-La Bassee Road	28/07/1917	31/07/1917
War Diary	Trenches S of La Bassee Road to Billets in Sailly La Bourse	31/07/1917	31/07/1917
Miscellaneous	Order for relief on Night of 19-20 by St. G Pousouby by I.M.C D.S.O.		
Miscellaneous			
Miscellaneous	Appendices.		
Miscellaneous	4th Corps No. 378 (G) 1st Division	17/07/1915	17/07/1915
Miscellaneous	Cold Gds	15/07/1915	15/07/1915
Miscellaneous	Head Quarters, IVth Corps	13/07/1915	13/07/1915
Miscellaneous	Village Fighting		
Miscellaneous	Concealment of movements of Troops and Traffic towards the Front		

1ST DIVISION

1ST BATTALION

COLDSTREAM GUARDS

AUG-DEC 1914

1914 AUG – 1915 JULY

TO GUARDS DIV

1st Guards Brigade.

1st Division.

1st BATTALION

COLDSTREAM GUARDS

AUGUST 1 9 1 4

Compiled by [illegible] Capt & Adjt. War Diary (from various sources)

1st Bn Coldstream Guards. 1st (Guards) Bde

Army Form C. 2118.

WAR DIARY
or
INTELLIGENCE SUMMARY

Hour, Date, Place.		Summary of Events and Information.	Remarks and ~~references~~ to Appendices.
Aug 13. 1914	FARNBORO	Embarked S.S. DUNVEGAN Castle at SOUTHAMPTON	All detailed records, orders etc for this period were lost during the days Octr 29th – Nov. 2nd 1914.
– 14 –		Disembarked at LE HAVRE.	
– 15 –	Rest Camp – LE HAVRE.		
– 16 –	LE. HAVRE	Entrained & via ROUEN, AMIENS, ARRAS to LA NOUVION. Billeted at LA NOUVION	
– 17 –	BOUÉ	Marched to BOUÉ, billeted.	
– 18 –	"	Billeted at BOUÉ.	
– 19 –	"		
– 20 –	"		
– 21 –	BOUÉ	Marched to CARTIGNES: billeted.	
– 22 –	CARTIGNES.	Marched to VIEUX RENG: billeted.	
– 23. –	VIEUX RENG	Marched to ROUVEROY – crossing frontier into BELGIUM	
– 24 –	ROUVEROY	Covered retirement of 3rd Brigade. RETREAT begins. Marched through MAUBEUGE to LA LONGUEVILLE. Billeted at LA LONGUEVILLE.	
– 25 –	LA LONGUEVILLE	Marched to DOMPIERRE: billeted	
– 26 –	DOMPIERRE	Marched to point 157 (2 miles E.N.E. of FAVRIL) and entrenched. Marched to FESMY: Billeted.	

Instructions regarding War Diaries and Intelligence Summaries are contained in F. S. Regs., Part II. and the Staff Manual respectively. Title pages will be prepared in manuscript.

WAR DIARY
or
INTELLIGENCE SUMMARY.
(*Erase heading not required.*)

Army Form C. 2118.

Place	Date	Hour	Summary of Events and Information	Remarks and references to Appendices
			C O P Y	
FESMY	27th	August 1914	Marches to ETREUX - deployed to defend Canal bridges. Retired without loss on GUISE. Marched to JANQUEUSE;billetted.	
JANQUEUSE	28th	"	Marched to ST GOBAIN; Billetted.	
ST GOBAIN	29th	"	Rested.	
"	30th	"	Marched to PINON; billetted.	
PINON	31st	"	Marched to MISSY; bivouacked	

(A9475) Wt W2358/P360 600,000 12/17 D. D. & L. Sch. 52a. Forms/C2118/15.

1st Guards Brigade.

1st Division.

1st BATTALION

COLDSTREAM GUARDS

SEPTEMBER 1 9 1 4

Attached is report on action 14.9.14.

[illegible]

1st Bn. Coldstream Guards

Army Form C. 2118.

WAR DIARY
or
INTELLIGENCE SUMMARY

1st (Guards) Bde

Hour, Date, Place.			Summary of Events and Information.	Remarks and ~~references~~ to Appendices.
27th	August 1914.	FESMY	Marched to ETREUX – deployed to defend canal bridges: retired without loss on GUISE. Marched to JANQUEUSE: billeted	
28th	–	– JANQUEUSE.	Marched to St GOBAIN: billeted.	
29th	–	– St. GOBAIN.	Rested.	
30th	–	– "	Marched to PINON: billeted.	
31st	–	– PINON	Marched to MISSY: bivouaced.	
1st	Septr.	1914. MISSY	Marched to LA FERTÉ-MILON: bivouaced.	
2nd	–	– LA FERTÉ-MILON	Marched to CHAMBRY: bivouaced.	
3rd	–	– CHAMBRY.	Marched to JOUARRE: bivouaced.	
4th	–	– JOUARRE	Marched to COULOMMIERS: billeted in the prison.	
5th	–	– COULOMMIERS	Marched to NESLES: billeted.	1st Reinforcement joined – Lieut. R. Wavell-Paxton and 90 other ranks.
6th	–	– NESLES.	ADVANCE begins. Marched to VOINSLES – through ROZOY – and took up a position there on receiving a report from a Sergeant of 15th Hsrs. at about 10 a.m. 1st Battn. C.G. formed Advanced Guard to 1st Divn. Ordered to retire to cross roads E. of ROZOY – advance continued in late afternoon to PUISEAU. (1½ miles N.E. of VOINSLES.): bivouaced.	Losses – Killed. 5 other ranks. Wounded. 4 officers – 33 other ranks. CAPT. E.G. Christie-Miller. Lieut. E.D.H. Tollemache. 2nd Lt. Hon. G.P.M.N. Sturt. 2nd Lt. F.C.R. Britten.

Army Form C. 2118.

1st Bn Coldstream Guards.

WAR DIARY or INTELLIGENCE SUMMARY 1st (Guards) Bde.

Hour, Date, Place.		Summary of Events and Information.	Remarks and ~~references to~~ Appendices.
7th Sept. 1914	PUISEAU.	Marched to LE TEMPLE (2 miles W. of LA FERTÉ-GAUCHER). Bivouaced.	
8th Sept. 1914	LE TEMPLE.	Advanced under intermittent long-range artillery fire to a point 1 mile E. of BASSEVELLE: bivouaced.	One shrapnel shell burst near Stretcher-bearers killing 5 & wounding the M.O. and 6 other ranks. No other casualties - Artillery formation adopted with success.
9th Sept. 1914.	Nr. BASSEVELLE	Marched due N. bivouaced near LUCY-le-bocage.	1st Draft joined early morning. Lieut. A.W.G. Campbell and 88 other ranks.
10th - -	Nr. Lucy-le-bocage	Marched to LATILLY: bivouaced.	
11th - -	LATILLY	Marched to BRUYÈRES: billeted	
12th - -	BRUYÈRES.	Marched to BAZOCHES: bivouaced.	
13th - -	BAZOCHES	Marched through BOURG to near MOULINS (N. of R. AISNE) and bivouaced about 11 p.m.	
14th - -	BATTLE of the AISNE.	All detailed reports, orders etc were lost during period Oct. 29th - Nov 2nd. The Battalion acted as advanced Guard to the Division and was directed to move N. over high ground between VENDRESSE and PAISSY finally reaching and taking CERNY-en-laonnois, from which a retirement was ordered after dusk. The final position held being on the spurs running N.E. from VENDRESSE and PAISSY. The Battalion was relieved and	KILLED. 11 other ranks. WOUNDED. 10 officers. 180 other ranks. MISSING. 1 officer 162 other ranks. WOUNDED. Lt. Col. J. PONSONBY. D.S.O. Major C.J.C. GRANT Captn G.H. BROWN. Captn G.J. EDWARDS Lieut. G.K.F. SMITH Lt. J.B.S. BOURNE-MAY Lt. D.M. HALL 2Lt. G.R. LANE 2nd Lt. Hon. D. BROWNE 2nd Lt. C.E. TUFNELL MISSING 2nd Lt. Hon G. FREEMAN-THOMAS

Army Form C. 2118.

1st Bn Coldstream Guards.

WAR DIARY
or
INTELLIGENCE SUMMARY

1st (Guards) Bde

Hour, Date, Place.		Summary of Events and Information.	Remarks and ~~references to~~ Appendices.
14th Septr 1914	AISNE (Continued)	Withdrew behind (S. of) VENDRESSE during the night.	
15th Septr 1914	VENDRESSE	In reserve.	
16th - -	do	ditto.	
17th - -	do	do	JOINED. Major. H. W STUDD. " J. STEELE. Captn A.G.E. EGERTON.
18th - -	do	Moved on to a portion of the position near TROYON and occupied the trenches relieving Bn Queen's W. Surrey.	KILLED. One. other ranks. Died of WOUNDS. Captn W.A. FULLER MAITLAND. Lieut A.W.G. CAMPBELL.
19th - -	TROYON ridge	Heavy firing but no more of importance on this front. 1st Brigade relieved & retired to OEUILLY to rest.	WOUNDED. Captn A.G.E. EGERTON & 17 other ranks.
20th - -	OEUILLY.	Resting.	JOINED. LIEUT. VISCOUNT ACHESON. " The Hon. C. DOUGLAS PENNANT. 218 other ranks.
21st - -	OEUILLY.	Moved into Brigade Support near VERNEUIL.	
22nd - -	VERNEUIL.	Same.	
23rd - -	VERNEUIL.	Moved into front line trenches at FERME de METZ 1 mile W.N.W. from VERNEUIL, relieving 1st Bn Scots Guards: the right of the Bn. resting on the OISE—AISNE canal.	
24th - -	Ferme de METZ.	Same	

Compiled by [illegible] (from [illegible])

1st Bn. Coldstream Guards.

Army Form C. 2118.

WAR DIARY
or
INTELLIGENCE SUMMARY

1st (Guards) Bde

Hour, Date, Place.		Summary of Events and Information.	Remarks and ~~references~~ to Appendices.
25th Septr 1914.	Ferme de METZ.	Heavy bombardment.	22 Casualties – other ranks.
26th - -	do	Heavy bombardment. 1st Bde relieved at night and retired to OEUILLY to rest.	WOUNDED. LIEUT. VISCOUNT ACHESON and 7 other ranks.
27th - -	OEUILLY.	At about 7 p.m. the 1st Bde was ordered to reoccupy TROYON ridge.	
28th Sept – 14th Octr 1914	N. of TROYON.	During this period the 1st Bn Coldstream Guards held a front with 2 companies remaining 2 companies in Support (in dug-outs). Reliefs were carried out every night. The daily bombardment was not usually directed at the trenches which suffered only slightly – the bulk of German shells being directed against our Artillery or Communication in rear. The weather was invariably good. On Oct. 4th 1914 one platoon of No. 2 Coy led by 2nd Lt. M.B. SMITH rushed with the bayonet and cleared an advanced German trench within 100x of our line. This was extremely well carried out and completely successful.	KILLED 7 other ranks. DIED of WOUNDS – 3 other ranks. WOUNDED. MAJOR. H.W. STUDD " J. STEELE. 2nd Lt. M.B. SMITH 56 other ranks. Missing 2 " "

1st Bn. COLDSTREAM GDS 1

Sept 14th, 1914.

On the morning of Sept 14th, after biovacing near PAISSY the Bn. was ordered to form the Advance Gd to the 1st Bde marching by MOULIN and VENDRESSE on CERNY at 6-45 AM.

Upon reaching VENDRESSE we found the 2nd Bde outposts engaged with the enemy; after passing VENDRESSE at Pt. A on map, the Bn. was ordered by Brigadier to move thro' woods on to high ground & move Northwards along the ridge towards CERNY. The Bn. deployed with Nos 4 & 1 Coys in firing line & 2 & 3 Coys in support; upon reaching the high ground we came under rifle fire from the direction of the factory & W. of it.

The 2 Coys. in support were soon brought into the firing line & the centre of the Bn. was directed

57

2

on the factory with the Cameron H.
on our left.
We, then, came under a very heavy rifle & shell fire and the sunken road at the factory was reached by short rushes with considerable loss.
The Bn. from this point became divided, No 3 Coy & part of No 2 Coy under Maj. Hon. L. Hamilton crossed the sunken road & swung round Northwards to the CHEMIN DES DAMES where they prolonged the right of a coy. of 4th Bn. K.R.R. under Major JELF. (See Map position B)
Here they remained fighting throughout the day, although on occasions owing to retirement of our line W. of Factory they were forced to retire to position C by high bank.
At dusk under orders of the Brigadier this portion of the Bn. was ordered to withdraw & re organize at P.D.

58

The other portion of the Bn. numbering 3
about 150 composed of Nos 2 & 4 Coys
under Lt Col J. Ponsonby became
divided from the remainder at
the factory, which was originally
occupied by the M. Gun section of
the R. Sussex.
When the Chimney fell this party
pushed forward under very severe
shell fire to a sunken road
running N. into CERNY which
was found to be unoccupied.
Maj Grant was ordered to go
round E. side of village, while
Col. Ponsonby pushed through
with the remainder, but touch
was lost & never regained,
Maj. Grant eventually rejoining
Maj. Hamilton's party. (6pm)
When Col Ponsonby's party
reached the N. edge of village
3 Coys of German Infantry were
seen on the ridge $\frac{1}{2}$ mile N.E
of village & other Germans

4.

on the ridge N W of village.

Col Ponsonby & his party pushed on & 6 M Gun Limbers were surprised, the horses of 4 of which were shot.

They afterwards pushed on into a small plantation (shown on sketch of Capt Warde Aldam's) which was reached about 10-15 AM where the Col was wounded, the party then remained hidden till mid-night when they rejoined as shown on ~~from~~ sketch. (The account of Col Ponsonby's party was taken from Capt Warde Aldam who was present with Col from early in the morning.)

N. of TROYON.
29. 9. 14.

61

Col. Ponsonby wounded at 10.15 a.m.

PLANTATION

thick wood

CERNY

Sunken road

Retire route at right

CHEMIN DE DAMES

9 a.m.

FACTORY

VENDRESSE

6.30 a.m.

Rough sketch of battle of CERNY
shewing my route in blue pencil
not drawn to scale.

W. St. A. Warde-Aldam
Capt
1 Batt. Coldstream Gds

62

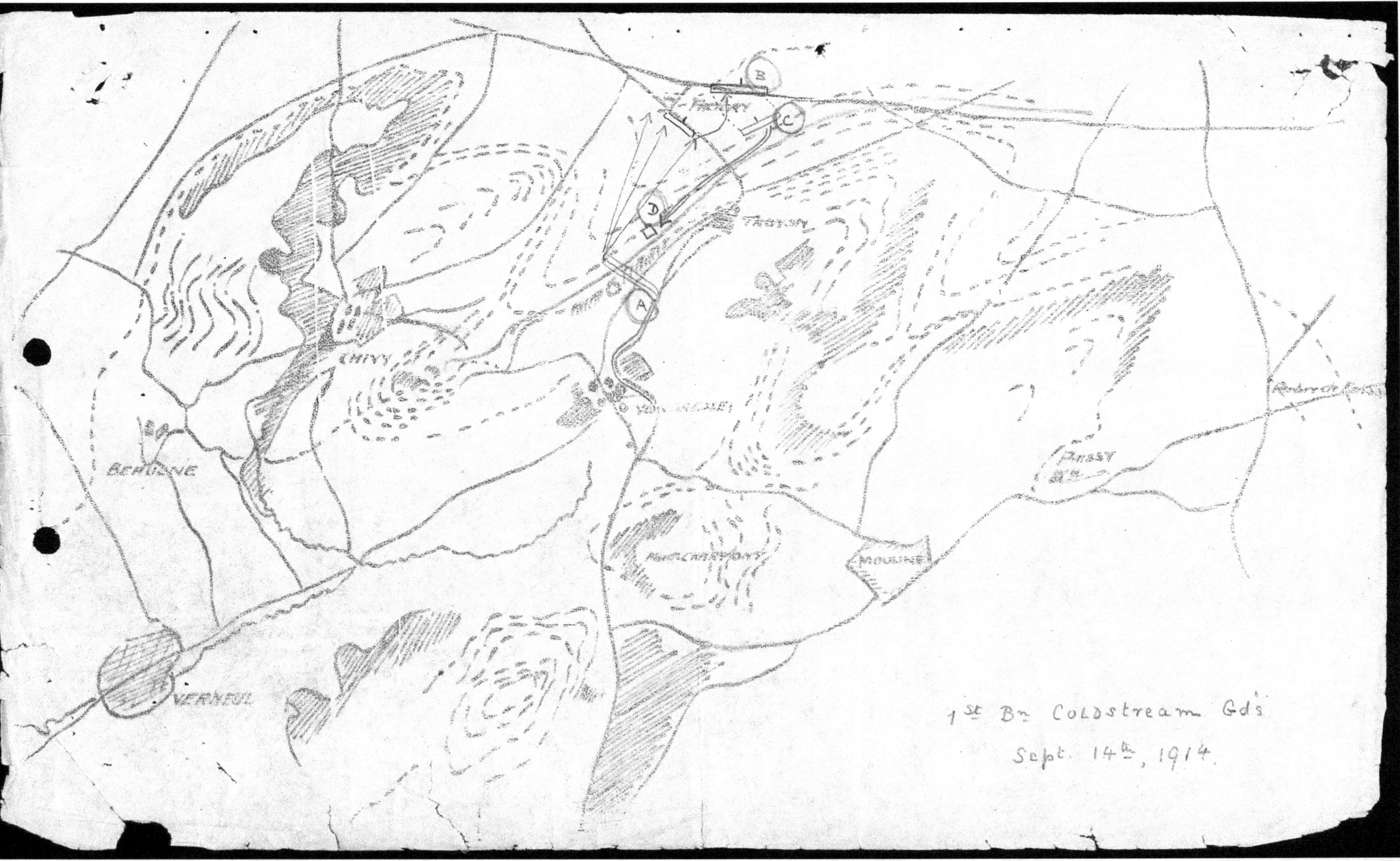

B
C
D
A
TROYON
CHIVY
BEAULNE
VERNEUIL
MOULINS
PAISSY
1st Bn Coldstream Gds
Sept. 14th, 1914

GSO II Grade 1st Division

Dear Parley [?]

Although I cannot say anything about the III Bde on the 14th, I send you direct a short account of what occurred near me with the 1st Bde, which may clear up the movements of part of the 1 CG.

On leaving the VENDRESSE-TROYON road the 1/CGs went to the left and eventually reached the top of the wood on the track running SW through the N of TROYON. The objective given to the companies attacking was the factory chimney and about 20 min after the attack began [times see 1/CGs account] the leading companies had reached the factory in the mist. At that time OC No 2 Co received a message from his Captain that there was a good position through the factory. Two platoon commanders had already been hit, but he pushed forward with every available man to the far side of the factory. There he found about 50-100 men and heard that a section had pushed into CERNY which was clear of the enemy. At that time OC 1/CGs arrived and the men there [about 150 belonging to two companies] pushed forward to road junction just S of CERNY, about 9 am. On arriving there OC 1st CGds pushed on through the village whilst OC 2 Co 1/CGs with 1 platoon went down the sunken lane to the right, and up into a field by the village to get round the right.

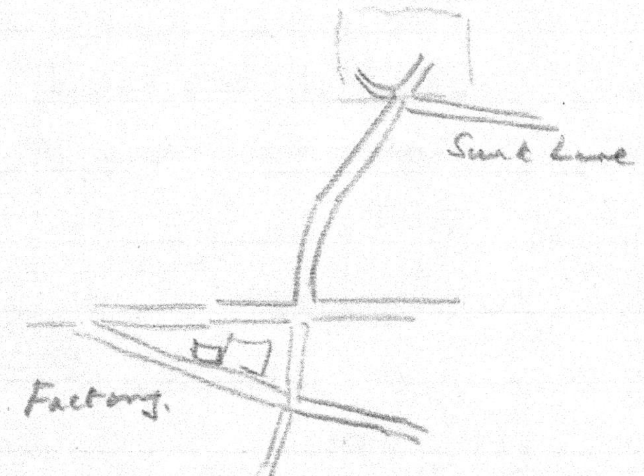

There were about 30 men of the 2nd Bde with whom he got touch and 1 platoon 1CG lined the lane. On looking through the mist, about 300 Germans could be seen retreating from the right rear, & going N.

The OC 2G ran back and sent a verbal message by an officer to the OC 1CG and a written message to 1st Bde HQrs to say that 1CG were pushing forward through CERNY and ~~being~~ that the enemy were on the right of the village retreating. By the time this message had been written all the 1CG, with OC 1CG (50 to 60 men) had pushed through the village and although OC 2G walked through the whole village twice at an interval of about an hour, not a sign of anyone could be found there. Eventually it was seen that the ~~Ge~~ English on both flanks were moving back towards the South, and after a certain delay the men in the road S of CERNY, 1 platoon 1 CG and 20 – 30 men Sussex and other Batns were taken back to the factory. There it was seen that the Germans on the left were already across the CHEMIN DES DAMES road on the South. OC No 2 Co 1 CG then collected every available man, formed them up behind a bank about the E of TROYON, and about 11.30 am counter attacked NW on the left of the II Bde. On reaching a line about between the factory and the battery (Maj Nicholson's) he found himself with about 1 officer 2nd Bde and some 30 to 40 men. They remained firing at the Germans advancing on to the CHIVY valley and protecting the right of the Guns till about 3pm dwindling in numbers. All messages to the rear having failed OC No 2 Co 1 CG took the opportunity about 3pm of going himself to get reinforcements, and on reaching the bank he had started from, he found some 200 – 300 under OC Sussex Regt, who at once pushed forward to reinforce the few men still left on the left. The situation was then reported by OC 2 Co 1/C Gds to Gen Balfour whom he found on the VENDRESSE CERNY road.

as regards CERNY the ground drops almost precipitately beyond the village into a very deep hollow and on the left the road is commanded by some high ground about the 1st P of CEMAE.

The confusion of units was probably due to the haste we started in and the casualties amongst officers. I lost 2 platoon commanders in the first 10 minutes and subsequently a third, and had to command the remains of his platoon together with any one I could find for the rest of the day.

Please forgive this scrawl. It may be quite useless. J. Ponsonby as you know eventually got back with about 50 men in the evening.

Yours

Charles Fraser.

29/9/14

No 2 Coy C. Gds.

1st Div. Vol II
Appendix XIX

(119)

Cerny-en-Laonnois

Chemin des Dames

2nd Bde

Fish Hook Trench

60 yds Coldstream Advanced Post

Troyon

1st Bde

60 +

Coldstream Observation Post

Strength.

1 platoon. assaulting party supported by another platoon & 2 sections machine guns.

Charles Corkran Major for G.O.C.

4.9.14. 1.30 pm

I consider this attack absolutely necessary
Chitham

Wt. W1154/2240. 7/11. 7,500,000. Sch. 4a. "A" Form. Army Form C. 2121.

MESSAGES AND SIGNALS.

No. of Message

Prefix ... Code ... m.	Words	Charge	This message is on a/c of: 1st Bde / C.D. Service.	Recd. at ... m.
Office of Origin and Service Instructions.	Sent			Date
	At ... m.			From
	To			
	By		(Signature of "Franking Officer.")	By

TO: 1st Division (Cameron) — 29 SEPT 14

Sender's Number.	Day of Month	In reply to Number	AAA
28.	29th Sept	G.84 of 28.9.14.	

I forward herewith reports of OC 1st Bn Coldstm & 1st Bn Camerons.

The Scots Gds & Black Watch were in reserve & their reports are not forwarded as they would not include any points you ask for.

If I may suggest it, can the reports forwarded stand over until the report by Major General Maxse is received from home?

Charles Corkran
Major
for G.O.C. 1st G. Bde

From: 1st Bgde.
Place
Time

The above may be forwarded as now corrected. (Z)

Censor. Signature of Addressor or person authorised to telegraph in his name.

* This line should be erased if not required.

Sept [?]

Bekynyton [?]
Farnham Royal
Bucks
16 Novr /24

Dear Edmonds

The following, which I have just come across in the private diary of Capt C. J. Balfour Scots Guards may interest you. Balfour was wounded on 13th Sept 1914 & was in hospital in Paris on 22nd when he writes.

"John Ponsonby (Col 1st Coldstreams) is here. He came & sat on my bed and told me what had happened to him on Monday 14th.
His adventures were as follows.
He had two companies in the firing line. He was the left company & went along to the other; he was knocked over twice by lyddite (Dirty Chartees (sic)) but was unhurt. He then reached the other company who were lining a wall near a factory chimney; some German shells then brought the factory chimney down on them. This was too hot a corner so John determined to go down a road close by. So with a company & and odd lot of men (10 Camerons & an officer, 9 Black Watch, some Scots (guards) & a few Cold-stream Guards) numbering about 50 he went down a road. There then came a fork in the road so John told the company to go down one and the 50 men went down the other.
On approaching a village* they were signalled to come forward by two men who were about 50 yards ahead acting as advance guard. On going up they found about 2 Bn of Germans having dinners in the middle of the street, so they wiped them out and took about 5 machine guns. There an officer with a red cross on his arms, covered with medals & decorations & followed by about 40 medical officers, came out of a big house and asked him to spare the house as they had got over 1000 wounded. So he assured the M.O that he meant him no harm. They then found out that they were surrounded so bolted for a wood. There they found a ditch with a hedge

*? Cerny
~~J.E.E.~~
As you know, it is a little way down the Ailette side, defiladed from the plateau & suitable for an advanced dressing station.
J.E.E.

in front - Here they ~~sat~~ lay surrounded on three sides by a German Army Corps (sic) - They gave all their ammunition but 10 rounds per man to one man who was a marksman the Germans shot at them for 7 hours (2 Bns) but whenever one of them showed himself the marksman had him so they never attempted to close - At dark the Germans ceased and calm reigned - John had been wounded in the ankle when they got into the ditch -
They then saw the German carts with dead & wounded go past them - Then a Brigade came & bivouacked the other side of the hedge & posted outpost sentries -
John & his men did not hardly dare breathe - At length at 12 midnight an awful gale sprang up and thereby made a great noise by rustling the trees - So taking advantage they crawled up the ditch, dodged the sentries & got back to their own lines, four men carrying John who was the only one of the party hit."
I don't know if this Col Ponsonby is alive but I daresay you do -

Yours sincerely
F. Loraine Petre

1st Guards Brigade.

1st Division.

<u>1st BATTALION</u>

<u>THE COLDSTREAM GUARDS</u>

<u>OCTOBER 1 9 1 4</u>

Army Form C. 2118.

Instructions regarding War Diaries and Intelligence Summaries are contained in F. S. Regs., Part II, and the Staff Manual respectively. Title pages will be prepared in manuscript.

WAR DIARY
or
INTELLIGENCE SUMMARY.
(Erase heading not required.)

COPY

Place	Date	Hour	Summary of Events and Information	Remarks and references to Appendices
28th September to 14th October 1914				
N. of TROYON.			During this period the 1st Battalion Coldstream Guards held a front with 2 Companies remaining 2 Companies in Support (in dug-outs). Reliefs were carried out every night. The daily bombardment was not usually directed at the trenches which suffered only slightly - the bulk of the German shells being directed against our Artillery or Communications in rear.	
			The weathwr was invariably good.	
			On October 4th 1914 one platoon of No. 2 Company led by 2/lt. M.B.Smith rushed with the bayonet and cleared an advanced German trench within 100x of our line. Tgis was extremely well carried out and completely successful.	

(A9475) Wt W2358/P360 600,000 12/17 D. D. & L. Sch. 52a. Forms/C2118/15.

Compiled by John Beckwith capt. & adjt.

1st Bn. Coldstream Guards

Army Form C. 2118.

WAR DIARY
or
INTELLIGENCE SUMMARY

1st (Guards) Bde

Hour, Date, Place.		Summary of Events and Information.	Remarks and ~~references~~ to Appendices.
15th Oct 1914.	TROYON.	Relieved by the French and moved to BLANZY-les-FISMES - arriving the following morning.	1.C.G.
16th Oct. 1914.	BLANZY.	Billeted.	
17th - -	BLANZY.	Moved to FISME and entrained there - [route via PARIS, BOULOGNE, and] HAZEBROUCK.	
18th - -	HAZEBROUCK.	Billeted	Draft joined. Captn G.H. BROWN. Lieut. C.J. MURRAY and 142 other ranks. 2nd Lieut. the Hon V. BOSCAWEN
19th - -	do	do	
20th - -	POPERINGHE.	Marched from HAZEBROUCK to POPERINGHE: billeted.	
21st - -	POPERINGHE	Marched via ELVERDINGHE, BOESINGHE to PILKELM. The 1st Bde ordered to attack in direction of LANGEMARCK - 1st Bn. C.G. in front line - 1st Bn the BLACK WATCH on left. 1st Bn Cameron Hghdrs - advanced guard & Cooperating. 1st Bn Scots Guards in reserve.	KILLED Lt F.R. POLLOCK + 30 other ranks. WOUNDED Captn G.M. PAGET + 92 other ranks. MISSING 73 other ranks.
Action at LANGEMARCK.		Armoured train covering advance from railway N. of & parallel to PILKEM-LANGEMARCK road.	
Note: All detailed records, orders etc were lost during period Oct 29 - Nov 2 1914.		Village of LANGEMARCK was secured and at night the line was made good up to the LANGEMARCK - BIXSCHOETE road.	
Oct 22nd 23rd ~~[illegible]~~ 1914	LANGEMARCK.	Action continued: Germans strongly entrenched.	

Compiled by Wm Beckwith Capt & adjt.

1st Bn. Coldstream Guards. Army Form C. 2118.

WAR DIARY
or
INTELLIGENCE SUMMARY

1st (Guards) Bde

Hour, Date, Place.		Summary of Events and Information.	Remarks and ~~references to~~ Appendices.
Oct 24th 1914.	LANGEMARCK	The French should have taken over the position at 7 p.m but were unable to approach owing to heavy bombardment.	1/B. G.
Oct 25th 1914.	LANGEMARCK	Relieved by the French at 7 a.m. and marched to just W. of ZILLIBEKE. Billeted at KLEIN ZILLIBEKE.	DRAFT officers joined 27.X.14 Capt. A.E. WATTS-RUSSELL, 2nd Lt. ALISON, 2nd Lt. WILLIAMS-WYNN. Joined 2.XI.14 Capt. E.G. CHRISTIE-MILLER, Capt. H.R.A. ADEANE, 186 other ranks.
Oct 26th – Action at GHELUVELT	Nr ZILLIBEKE. Halted	Moved along YPRES—MENIN Road to HOOGE and in action near GHELUVELT clearing woods on both sides of YPRES-MENIN road.	KILLED. 3: MAJOR the Hon L. d'H. HAMILTON M.V.O. (Commanding), CAPT H.R.A. ADEANE, Lieut. J. MURRAY
Oct 27th 1914	GHELUVELT	The advance being made during early hours of the day: Orders were received to advance on trenches held by our troops just W. of the BECELAERE—WERVICQ road with a view to an attack on the German trenches opposed to them. However at night the Battn. occupied a continuation of our trenches somewhat further N.	WOUNDED 2: CAPT. W. St A WARDE-ALDAM, Lieut. F W GORE-LANGTON.
28th Oct 1914	GHELUVELT	Held the above line of trenches.	MISSING 10: CAPT. E G. CHRISTIE-MILLER, CAPT. J. E. GIBBS, CAPT. G. H. BROWN, Lt. & adjt. G. A. CAMPBELL, Lieut. the Hon C. DOUGLAS-PENNANT, Lieut. R. WAVELL-PAXTON, Lieut. G. K. F. SMITH, 2nd Lt. the Hon. V. BOSCAWEN, 2nd Lt. WILLIAMS-WYNN, 2nd Lt. ALISON
29th Oct. 1914	do.	An attack by the Germans of which notice was received was beaten off at 5.30 a.m. in dense mist but was successful further S. at cross-roads E.S.E of GHELUVELT: the result being that the Battn. trenches were almost immediately afterwards attacked from the right rear. A retirement appears to have been ordered and a	

WAR DIARY
or
INTELLIGENCE SUMMARY.
(Erase heading not required.)

Instructions regarding War Diaries and Intelligence Summaries are contained in F. S. Regs., Part II. and the Staff Manual respectively. Title pages will be prepared in manuscript.

Place	Date	Hour	Summary of Events and Information	references to Appendices
GHELUVELT	29th October 1914		small portion of the Battalion re-formed covering the E. side of GHELUVELT village on the S. side of the YPRES-MENIN Road, covering a Battery R.F.A. . At night the battalion was withdrawn and bivouacke d in woods W.of GHELUVELT in Brigade Reserve.	
Nr. GHELUVELT	30th October 1914.		In Brigade Reserve between HOOGE & GHELUVELT	
do	31st do		dol do.	

(A9475) Wt W2358/P360 600,000 12/17 D. D. & L. Sch. 52a. Forms/C2118/15.

1

Confidential

Orders

1/ No 2 Coy will find One platoon, under 2 Lt M. BECKWITH SMITH, made up to 50 rifles to attack Enemy's advanced trench lying opposite the COLDSTREAM advanced post.

2/ The Platoon will assemble in the Coy lines at 7.30 p.m. and be moved into our trench (E. of FACTORY road). From there they will deploy just N. of the line of our high wire fence with their left on the sap leading to our advanced post & lie down. In moving out they must keep low. Dress for all ranks, Bandolier, rifle & bayonet. Bayonets will be fixed before leaving the trench and rifles will be carried at the trail, loaded with safety catches back.

3/ At 8 p.m. the advance in line will commence, the centre directing and marching on centre of German trench.
They will be careful that our left

extends as far as the flank of the German trench.

4 The nearest trench will be taken with the bayonet. When this is carried the platoon will advance & take ~~over~~ the second trench.

5 A party of 30 men, under a Sergt. to be detailed by O.C. 2 Coy, with a shovel each will be brought up to our trench (E. of FACTORY ROAD) behind the attacking platoon and will get into the trench as soon as the attacking platoon leaves it. Dress, Rifles slung & bandolier.

6 If 2 Lt M. B. Smith thinks it practicable he will after taking the second trench send for this party who will fill in the nearest trench.

7 A blast on the whistle will be the signal for ~~the~~ party to return to their trenches.

8 The Password which will be used by the men on returning to their trench will be COLDSTREAM.

9 Only the Officer and Platoon Sgt will carry whistles.

10 The Plan of attack will be explained carefully to all ranks & the whole operation will be carried out in <u>absolute</u> <u>silence</u> and the position of the moon at the time of the advance and any land mark likely to help men in keeping their direction both in advancing and returning will be pointed out to them.

11. A compass bearing will be taken from the point of departure to the centre of Enemy's trench.

L.M. Hamilton Major
Commanding
1st Battn Coldstream Gds.

4.10.14.

1 Cpl & 2 Sappers RE and the Shorts joined party OK

Report on attack on German "Fish-hook" Trench on the night of Oct. 4/5th 1914.

Orders for attack have already been sent you. In accordance with the orders No. 6 Platoon made up to 50 men by No. 8 Platoon under command of 2 Lt. M. Beckwith Smith were deployed clear of our trench by 7-45 p.m. and 30 men for digging with 1 Corpl & 2 men of the R.E. were ready in our trench. Shortly after, the order for the attacking platoon was given to advance. The first trench was occupied without any opposition and was found to be empty. About 15 Germans were lying dead in this trench probably killed by shell fire and our snipers on the 4th. After a short pause the advance was continued towards the second trench, about 70 yds. distant from the first, when about half-way to this trench a few shots were fired and 2 Lt. M. Beckwith Smith gave the order to charge.

The Officer led the charge and reached

the trench first closely followed by his platoon.

They jumped into the trench and bayonetted and shot all the Germans in it, about 20 in all.

2 Lt. M. B. Smith was knocked down in the struggle and shot through the arm. No 8085 A/L/Corpl. Russell bayonetted the two Germans who were attacking the officer, thereby saving the officer's life.

Fire was then opened by the Germans from a third trench and strong re inforcements were seen coming up.

Having complied with the first part of the orders issued to him, i.e. to take the first two trenches, it became evident that it would now be impossible to fill in the first trench, 2 Lt Smith therefore, gave the order to withdraw to our trenches in accordance with the orders he had received.

This withdrawal he successfully accomplished.

The Casualties were: Wounded –
1 officer – Other ranks 7.
Missing – Other ranks 2 (both these men were thought to have been killed in the German trenches).

3

I should like to bring to yr notice the excellent way in which 2 Lt M. B. Smith both arranged and carried out his mission

The following are also deserving of special mention –

No 7983 Sgt W. Brown & No 5018 acting Sgt G TROKE who behaved with great coolness and gave their officer every assistance.

No 8085 a/L/Cpl R. Russell mentioned above in my report.

No 8725 Pte R PAXTON who by his promptitude in the German trench was probably the means of saving Sgt. BROWN's life.

The first trench ~~appears~~ is reported to be a deep narrow trench giving cover standing and appears to be not yet completed. The Second trench has a still deeper part (cut out at the back) making the Section as shown.

There are recesses cut in under this trench for cover from Shell fire held up by props & boards.

-4'6"

-6'

E. M. Hamilton Major

5. 10. 14.

Commanding 1st BN. COLDM. GDS.

Copy.

VENDRESSE
Oct. 5th '14.

Headquarters,
1st Division

The attack on the enemy's advanced trenches was made last night Oct 4th. at 8 p.m. by a Platoon of the 1st Bn Coldstream Guards under the command of 2/Lt. M. Beckwith-Smith and was entirely successful.

The Trenches ordered to be attacked consisted of one long trench shaped like a fish hook, its right flank thrown back on to the sugar factory road whilst behind this trench are 3 others at no great distance one behind the other.

These trenches are very close to our main line of trenches and are probably observation posts for the enemy's artillery. I considered it a necessary duty to attack them.

I attach the orders for the operations by the O.C. 1/ Bn Coldstream Guards which explain what the attacking party was ordered to do.

2nd Lt. M. Beckwith Smith led the attack with great gallantry and carried the affair through with great coolness.

The front trench was successfully rushed as also the one immediately behind it. Owing to the rifle fire from the third trench the party intended for filling in the first trench was unable to do so except with great loss of life and the attacking party was ordered to withdraw

20 of the enemy were shot or bayonetted in the trenches whilst 2nd Lt. M. Beckwith Smith and 7 men were wounded and 2 men killed or missing.

I desire to mention specially in addition to 2nd Lt. Beckwith Smith, for coolness and gallantry

No. 7983 Sergt. W. Brown } who gave great assistance
" 5018 a/Sergt. G. Stoke } to the Officer.
" 8085 L/Cpl. R. Russell } who bayonetted 3 Germans who
" 8425 Pte R. Paxton } were attacking 2nd Lt. B. Smith.

The O.C. 1/Bn Coldstream Guards has been ordered to strengthen and extend his sap so that from a more advanced position he can make the enemy's advanced trenches as uncomfortable as possible.

A supply of rifle grenades is urgently required for this purpose as also iron or steel plates for strengthening loop holes – the ordinary sand bags at close range not being of much use.

(sd) C. Fitzclarence Br. Genl.
Cdg. 1st Guards Brigade

1st Guards Brigade.

1st Division.

1st BATTALION

THE COLDSTREAM GUARDS.

NOVEMBER 1 9 1 4

Completed by [illegible] Capt [illegible]

1st Bn Coldstream Guards.

Army Form C. 2118.

WAR DIARY
or
INTELLIGENCE SUMMARY

1st Guards Bde

Hour, Date, Place.		Summary of Events and Information.	Remarks and ~~references~~ to Appendices.
29th Oct 1914	GHELUVELT	Small portion of the Battn reformed covering the E. side of GHELUVELT village on the S. side of the YPRES – MENIN road, covering a battery R.F.A. At night the Battn was withdrawn and bivouaced in woods W. of GHELUVELT in Brigade reserve.	1. C. G.
30th Oct. 1914.	nr GHELUVELT.	In Brigade Reserve between HOOGE and GHELUVELT	Battalion fighting strength – 80, commanded by Lieut and Quarter Master J. Boyd.
31st Oct. 1914	do	do	
1st Nov. 1914	do.	do. [The] draft [2 officers + 66 O.R. mentioned in Col of remarks overleaf] joined at night.	Capt E. C. CHRISTIE-MILLER took over Command
2nd Nov. 1914	do.	Relieved 2 companies of 1st Bn The BLACK WATCH in trenches: During a German attack the line was again broken and losses amounted to 50% including both officers.	
3rd Nov. 1914	do	In Bde Reserve	Lt & Qr Mr J Boyd took over Command. Total ration strength – 240.
4th Nov. 1914	do	ditto	
5th Nov. 1914	do	Marched to Wood 1½ miles due N. of GHELUVELT and attached to 2nd Bn. Coldstream Guards.	Officers joined. Captn G. J. Edwards & took command. 2nd Lt. J. McNeile 2nd Lt B. D. TOLLEMACHE.

Compiled by : Wm Beckwith Capt. & Adjt.

1st Bn. Coldstream Guards.

Army Form C. 2118.

WAR DIARY
or
INTELLIGENCE SUMMARY

1st Guards Bde

Hour, Date, Place.		Summary of Events and Information.	Remarks and ~~references to~~ Appendices.
Nov. 6. 1914.	N. of GHELUVELT.	Attached 2nd Bn Coldstream Guards	
Nov. 7. 1914.	do.	do	Draft joined. 2nd Lt D. GLASS and 94 other ranks
Nov. 8th to 11th 1914.	do	do.	1. 6. G.
Nov. 12th 1914.	do.	Marched to ZONNEBEKE in support 5th Bde. Ceased to be attached to 2nd Bn. Coldstream Guards. Same night moved in support of 6th Bde.	
Nov. 13th to 15th 1914.	ZONNEBEKE.	Still in support of 6th Bde.	
Nov. 16th 1914	do.	Relieved by the French and bivouaced in a wood just N.W. of HOOGE until night when marched to N. of KLEIN ZILLIBEKE in support of the 2nd Bn Grenadier Guards (4th Guards Bde). Attached to 3rd Bn. Coldstream Gds.	
Nov. 17th to 19th 1914	N. KLEIN ZILLIBEKE.	Attached to 3rd Bn Coldstream Guards.	
Nov. 20th "	do.	1st Corps relieved by the French. Marched to METTEREN. Billeted.	
Nov 21st "	METEREN	Billetted.	
Nov. 22nd "	do	do	Lt Col. J PONSONBY D.S.O. returned to duty.
Nov. 23rd	do	Marched to STRAZEELE. Billetted.	
Nov. 24th – 27th	STRAZEELE	Billetted in STRAZEELE.	

Instructions regarding War Diaries and Intelligence Summaries are contained in F. S. Regs., Part II. and the Staff Manual respectively. Title pages will be prepared in manuscript.

WAR DIARY
or
INTELLIGENCE SUMMARY.
(Erase heading not required.)

Army Form C. 2118.

Place	Date	Hour	Summary of Events and Information	Remarks and references to Appendices
			COPY	
			November 1914	
			28th STRAZEELE F.M. Sir John French inspected and spoke to the battalion.	
			29th & 30 th " Billetted. D raft joined	
			C apt The Hon. J.B. Campbell 2nd Lt. G.C. Mills. 2nd L t. T.A. Tapp. 2nd Lt. E.A. Beauchamp	
			211 Other Ranks	

(A9475) Wt W2358/P360 600,000 12/17 D. D. & L. Sch. 52a. Forms/C2118/15.

1st Guards Brigade.

1st Division.

1st BATTALION

COLDSTREAM GUARDS

DECEMBER 1 9 1 4

Compiled by Wm Beckwith Capt 9 adjt.

1st Bn Coldstream Guards.

Army Form C. 2118.

WAR DIARY
or
INTELLIGENCE SUMMARY

1st Guards Bde

Hour, Date, Place.		Summary of Events and Information.	Remarks and ~~references to~~ Appendices.
Nov. 28th 1914.	STRAZEELE	F.M. Sir John French inspected & spoke to the Battn.	
" 29th & 30th 1914.	do	Billetted.	
Dec. 1st 1914	do	do.	DRAFT JOINED. CAPT. the HON. J. B. CAMPBELL, 2nd Lt. G. C. MILLS, 2nd Lt. T. A. TAPP, 2nd Lt. E. A. BEAUCHAMP } 211 other ranks
Dec. 2nd to 1914. Dec 12th	do	Reforming and training the Battalion.	H.M. the King inspected the Bn. 3. xii. 14.
Dec. 13th 1914.	do		DRAFT-JOINED. CAPT. G. STEWART. 2nd Lt. L. F. R. COLERIDGE. 2nd Lt. G. C. ARMSTRONG } 201 other ranks
Dec. 14th to 18th 1914.	do	do.	
Dec. 19th 1914.	do	do	Officers joined. CAPT. A. G. E. EGERTON, CAPT. W. H. BECKWITH (adjutant), 11 other ranks.
Dec. 20th 1914.	do.	Ordered to march at once - started at 5 p.m. via MERVILLE to BETHUNE: billetted in COLLEGE de Jeunes Filles. 20 miles - arrived 12 mn. Fine night - roads fair. 1 Sergeant & 6 men only fell out.	I. G. G.

Instructions regarding War Diaries and Intelligence Summaries are contained in F. S. Regs., Part II. and the Staff Manual respectively. Title pages will be prepared in manuscript.

WAR DIARY
or
INTELLIGENCE SUMMARY.
(Erase heading not required.)

Army Form C. 2118.

Hour, Date, Place	Summary of Events and Information	Remarks and references to Appendices
12 noon 21st Dec: 1914 BETHUNE	Bn marched with Brigade Camerons leading followed by COLDSTREAM to PONT FIXE, GIVENCHY. Bde orders issued en route to attack RUE d'OUVERT from PONT FIXE, cooperating if possible with 3rd Bde on the left. Bde attacked at 3pm COLDSTREAM & CAMERONS in first line.	
3 pm. PONT FIXE.	Bn attacked in the following order Nos: 2 & 3 coys: in 1st line, No 2 on right, No 3 on left, No: 4 coy in 2nd line, No 1 coy in support. A few shells caused one or two casualties in the village while crossing the PONT FIXE, with this exception the enemy's artillery fire caused no damage. As soon as attack started the leading coys: came under enfilade rifle & machine gun fire but owing to a heavy hailstorm which came on right in the enemy's face, casualties were not heavy.	1. 6. 9
4.30 pm. GIVENCHY	Nos: 2, 3 & 4 coys: occupied old French trenches on the reverse slope of the spur about 300 yds. W of the trenches evacuated by the Indian troops on the 19th inst: now held by the Germans. Lt Col: Ponsonby established his Hd. Qrs in the W end house of GIVENCHY VILLAGE & No 1 coy: was posted in trenches about the same place. ~~Capt. Daniels of the 15th Sikhs~~ A patrol under 2nd Lt Mills went forward to the end of GIVENCHY VILLAGE & reported it clear of the enemy as far as the CHURCH	
5 pm – 3 am	attempts to straighten up the line & get in touch with the GLOUCESTERS on the left & CAMERONS on the right, but proper touch could not be obtained.	
4 am	Lt Col. Ponsonby assisted by Capt Daniels 15th Sikhs made a reconnaissance & found a coy of LONDON SCOTTISH on the left rear of No 2 coy: which were almost immediately withdrawn.	
6.45 am. 22nd Dec 1914	The 3 coys in the forward trenches attacked the German trench along the road leading from GIVENCHY to CHAPELLE St ROCHE & took it but being without any support on their flanks they were bombed out of it about 8 am & retired having lost over 50% of their strength on to No 1 coy: posted to the W of the church. Bn Hd Qrs had been moved to the same place when the attack started.	

(73989) W4141—463. 400,000. 9/14. H.&J.Ltd. Forms/C. 2118/10.

Instructions regarding War Diaries and Intelligence Summaries are contained in F. S. Regs., Part II. and the Staff Manual respectively. Title pages will be prepared in manuscript.

WAR DIARY
or
INTELLIGENCE SUMMARY.
(*Erase heading not required.*)

Army Form C. 2118.

Hour, Date, Place	Summary of Events and Information	Remarks and references to Appendices
	The machine guns under Lt Tapp which had gone forward with the first line on the previous day were strongly posted at the corner of an orchard 100 yds N of 'FRENCH FARM' held by a French coy'. There was very little firing all day & the line of trenches was gradually consolidated by coys: from the London Scottish & Camerons. Lt Colonel Ponsonby told off 2Lt Armstrong to act as Adjutant for the night of the 21st–22nd. The Bn cooperated with the 83rd & 85th Bty R.F.A. during both attacks.	21st to 22nd Dec:
6 pm 22nd Dec: 1914	Lt Colonel Ponsonby having had a bad attack of fever handed over command to Capt A. Egerton but returned early next day & resumed command.	KILLED Capt: G. Stewart 9 other ranks
9 pm	Bn was relieved by Black Watch & marched back to billets in village south of canal at PONT FIXE.	DIED OF WOUNDS 2nd Lt C. A. Beauchamp 1 other ranks
23rd Dec: 1914. PONT FIXE.	In billets. Farm buildings round a dirty midden. Wet & cold.	WOUNDED 128 other ranks. WOUNDED & MISSING 2nd Lt J. McNeile 2nd Lt B. B. Tollemache (since found) 2nd Lt L. F. R. Coleridge (ditto MISSING 57 other ranks.

Instructions regarding War Diaries and Intelligence Summaries are contained in F. S. Regs., Part II. and the Staff Manual respectively. Title pages will be prepared in manuscript.

WAR DIARY
or
INTELLIGENCE SUMMARY.
(*Erase heading not required.*)

Army Form C. 2118.

Hour, Date, Place	Summary of Events and Information	Remarks and references to Appendices
23rd December 1914 GIVENCHY + CAMBRIN	The battalion moved back to billets near Cambrin A 20 b 1 8. In Brigade Reserve	
24th December 1914 CAMBRIN.	Battalion still in Brigade Reserve	
25th December 1914 "	Battalion still in Brigade Reserve. T.M. Christmas cards and Princess Marys gifts presented to N.C.O.s + men	
26th December 1914 CAMBRIN + GIVENCHY	The battalion moved up into the trenches at GIVENCHY	1 other rank wounded
27th December 1914 GIVENCHY		Killed Other ranks 1 Wounded Other ranks 1.
28th December 1914 " and billetted at BETHUNE	Batt^n left GIVENCHY and billetted at BETHUNE	Major Hon C. Willoughby Lt Hon D Browne 2Lieut Evan Thomas 2Lieut W.S Bosanquet and 102 other ranks joined
[illegible] December 1914 BETHUNE	Batt^n came in waiting at 6 pm ready to move at ½ hours notice	
30th December 1914 "	Draft inspected by C.O.	
[illegible] December 1914 [illegible] billetted at BEVRY	All N.C.O.s and men went to Divisional Swimming Bath. Batt^n marched to BEVRY and billetted, in Brigade Reserve	
[illegible]	Batt^n marched to ANNEQUIN and billetted, in Brigade Reserve	

1. 6. G.

H.&J.Ltd. Forms/C. 2118/10.

71

D. A.G.
3rd Echelon

Herewith War Diary of the 1st Bn Coldstream Guards up to and including the action at GIVENCHY on Dec 21st 1914.

All records of a detailed nature were lost during the period Oct 29th – Nov. 2nd 1914 – but only facts which can be strictly verified are recorded.

An accurate record begins from Dec 19th 1914 but the work entailed in compiling the earlier period has up to now interfered with the arrangement of events subsequent to that date.

C.M.H. Morton [illegible] Captain
Commdg 1st Bn Coldstream Guards.

26.2.15.

1ST DIVISION
1ST BRIGADE

1ST BATTALION .

COLDSTREAM GUARDS

JAN - JULY 1915

1st Division
1st Brigade

WAR DIARY

1st COLDSTREAM GUARDS

January

1 9 1 5

COPY. <u>Original in Diary for December 1914</u>

W A R   D I A R Y

<u>1st Coldstream Guards</u>

1st January 1915. & billetted at ANNEQUIN	Battalion marched to ANNEQUIN and billetted: in Brigade Reserve.

Army Form C. 2118.

Instructions regarding War Diaries and Intelligence Summaries are contained in F. S. Regs., Part II. and the Staff Manual respectively. Title pages will be prepared in manuscript.

WAR DIARY
or
INTELLIGENCE SUMMARY.

(*Erase heading not required.*)

Hour, Date, Place		Summary of Events and Information	Remarks and references to Appendices
2nd January 1915 and trenches at	ANNEQUIN GIVENCHY	The Battn marched from ANNEQUIN and went into the trenches at GIVENCHY	Wounded :- Other ranks 3
3rd January 1915	GIVENCHY		Wounded :- Other ranks 7
4th January 1915	"		Wounded :- Other ranks 2
5th January 1915	"		
6th January 1915	"		1/6 G
7th January 1915	"		
8th January 1915	"		Wounded :- Other ranks 2
9th January 1915	"		
10th January 1915			Wounded :- Other ranks 1

(73989) W4141—463. 400,000. 9/14. H.&J.Ltd. Forms/C. 2118/10.

Instructions regarding War Diaries and Intelligence Summaries are contained in F. S. Regs., Part II. and the Staff Manual respectively. Title pages will be prepared in manuscript.

WAR DIARY
or
INTELLIGENCE SUMMARY.

(Erase heading not required.)

Army Form C. 2118.

Hour, Date, Place		Summary of Events and Information	Remarks and references to Appendices
11th January 1915	GIVENCHY		Wounded Other ranks 3.
12th January 1915	"		Wounded Other ranks 3.
13th January 1915 and billetted at BETHUNE	"	The Battalion marched from GIVENCHY and billetted in [MONTMORENCY] BARRACKS BETHUNE	
14th January 1915	BETHUNE	The Commanding Officer inspected the billets	
15th January 1915	"	All N.C.O.s men had a bath at the Divisional Baths	Lieut Viscount Acheson and 2/Lt W. S. Scott Elliott joined
16th January 1915	"	Route march under Company arrangements. Battalion in waiting from 6pm ready to move at 1 hours notice	2/Lieuts G.N. Clifton, H.W. Clifton and J.S. Spencer joined
17th January 1915	"	Battalion paraded for Divine Service at 10.45am	
18th January 1915	"	Recruiting parade held at 7.30am. Short route march under Coy arrangements was carried out also 1 hours musketry	
19th January 1915	"	3 companies bathed at the Divisional Baths and at the disposal of Company officers	2/Lieuts J. Coats and R.M. Wright 166 other ranks joined
20th January 1915		Draft inspected by the Commanding Officer. No 4 Coy bathed at the Divisional Baths. Training of bomb throwers	

(73989) W4141—463. 400,000. 9/14. H.&J.Ltd. Forms/C. 2118/10.

Instructions regarding War Diaries and Intelligence Summaries are contained in F. S. Regs., Part II. and the Staff Manual respectively. Title pages will be prepared in manuscript.

WAR DIARY
or
INTELLIGENCE SUMMARY.
(Erase heading not required.)

Army Form C. 2118.

Hour, Date, Place	Summary of Events and Information	Remarks and references to Appendices
21st January 1915 BETHUNE and billetted at CAMBRIAN	The G.O.C 1st Corps inspected the Battalion. After the inspection the Battalion marched to CAMBRIAN in Brigade Reserve	
22nd January 1915 CAMBRIAN	In Brigade Reserve. The billets were bad - most of the houses were in ruins with no roofs or walls left	2 Lieut J.E. Rodgers joined
23rd January 1915 CAMBRIAN and trenches at CUINCHY	The Battalion left CAMBRIAN and went into the trenches at CUINCHY relieving the London Scottish - Trenches had not been completed communication trenches bad and fire trenches full of water heavy rain all night.	
24th January 1915 CUINCHY	The Germans shelled the position most of the day with their heavy guns - most of the fire being directed on Pont Fixe. Impossible for working parties to be employed on improving the trenches	Killed: Other ranks 1 Wounded: Other ranks 5
25th January 1915 CUINCHY	about 7 am a German deserter came in and reported an attack imminent - The German attack commenced by the explosion of a mine in the trench held by No 4 Coy under Capt Campbell - The first line of trenches were consequently rushed by the Germans - No 1 Coy on the embankment by the La Bassee Canal held its ground and No 2 Coy under Lt Visc Acheson held on to the Keep and Brick stacks and repelled the German attacks - The Scots Guards on our immediate right shared a similar fate but were able to maintain a stand at the Brickfields Reinforcements of London Scottish Black Watch and Cameron Highlanders were sent up and a counter attack was made but it was found impossible	Killed: 2 Lieut C.H. Mills Died of Wounds. 2 Lieut J.E. Rodgers Wounded. 2 Lieut R.M. Wright 2 Lieut C.N. Clifton 2 Lieut T.A. Tapp 2 Lieut J.B. Coote Missing Capt C.K. Hutchison Capt Hon J.B. Campbell 2 Lieut G. Armstrong 2 Lieut H.N. Clifton Killed: Other ranks 19 Died of wounds Other ranks 1 Wounded: Other Ranks 54 Missing: Other Ranks 118

Army Form C. 2118.

Instructions regarding War Diaries and Intelligence Summaries are contained in F. S. Regs., Part II. and the Staff Manual respectively. Title pages will be prepared in manuscript.

WAR DIARY
or
INTELLIGENCE SUMMARY.
(Erase heading not required.)

Hour, Date, Place	Summary of Events and Information	Remarks and references to Appendices
25th Jan 1915 CUINCHY	to dislodge the Germans from the front trenches they had taken – Major Hon C Willoughby took over the command during the day from Lt Col Ponsonby (admitted subsequently to Hospital with Bronchitis) – The Batt remained in position during the night of Jan 25th	

(73989) W4141—463. 400,000. 9/14. H.&J.Ltd. Forms/C. 2118/10.

Instructions regarding War Diaries and Intelligence Summaries are contained in F. S. Regs., Part II. and the Staff Manual respectively. Title pages will be prepared in manuscript.

WAR DIARY
or
INTELLIGENCE SUMMARY.

(*Erase heading not required.*)

Army Form C. 2118.

Hour, Date, Place	Summary of Events and Information	Remarks and references to Appendices
26th January 1915 CUINCHY and billetted at BETHUNE	The Battalion left the trenches at CUINCHY and billetted at BETHUNE	2 Lieuts Hon C.R. Digby, C.E. G Green, C.K. Stephenson and 110 other ranks join
27th January 1915 BETHUNE	Battalion parade in Marching Order at 10.30am	
28th January 1915 "	Companies paraded in clean fatigue dress and rifles. Battalion in waiting from 6pm, ready to move at 1 hours notice	
29th January 1915 "	Battalion paraded for a route march under Coy Officers at 9am.	
30th January 1915 " and billetted at OBLINGHAM	Battalion paraded at 9am for a route march, also at 2.30pm and marched to OBLINGHAM to billets	
31st January 1915 OBLINGHAM and billetted at ECQUEDECQUES	Battalion paraded at 12.45pm and marched to ECQUEDECQUES to billets	
1st February 1915 ECQUEDECQUES	Companies at disposal of Company Officers - 1 hours musketry to be done	
2nd February 1915 "	Companies at disposal of Company Officers all day	
3rd February 1915 "	Company Training under Company Commanders	
4th February 1915 "	Company Training under Company Commanders. Training of snipers and bomb-throwers carried out	

(73989) W4141—463. 400,000. 9/14. H.&J.Ltd. Forms/C. 2118/10.

1st Division
1 Brigade

WAR DIARY

1st COLDSTREAM GUARDS

February

1 9 1 5

War Diary (Copy) — 1st Coldstream Guards.

1st February 1915	ECQUEDECQUES	Companies at disposal of Company Officers – 1 hours musketry to be done.
2nd February 1915	"	Companies at disposal of Company Officers all day.
3rd February 1915	"	Company training under Company Commanders.
4th February 1915	"	Company training under Company Commanders. Training of Snipers and bomb-throwers carried out.

Instructions regarding War Diaries and Intelligence Summaries are contained in F. S. Regs., Part II. and the Staff Manual respectively. Title pages will be prepared in manuscript.

WAR DIARY

or

INTELLIGENCE SUMMARY.

(*Erase heading not required.*)

Army Form C. 2118.

Hour, Date, Place		Summary of Events and Information	Remarks and references to Appendices
5th February 1915	ECQUEDECQUES	Company Training from 9am till 12 noon and from 2pm till 4pm All Officers and Sergeants paraded at the Orderly Room for a lecture by the C.O. at 6pm	
6th February 1915	"	Company Training under Company Commanders. Class of Instruction for corporals at 6pm nightly in the Orderly Room commenced.	
7th February 1915	"	Battalion paraded for Divine Service at 1.15pm	Lieut Hon JCB Agar-Robartes, 2 Lieut Hon C.H.F. Noel and 160 other ranks join
8th February 1915	"	Draft inspected by C.O. Company Training under Company Commanders.	
9th February 1915	"	2 Companies Route Marching 2 Companies Musketry	
10th February 1915	"	Companies paraded at 8.30am for a route march. Instruction in trench mortar given to 160 men by the RFA.	
11th February 1915	"	2 Companies Musketry 2 Companies Route Marching	
12th February 1915	"	2 Companies Rifle range 2 Companies Route marching	
13th February 1915	"	2 Companies instruction in wire entanglements by the RE 2 Companies musketry	
14th February 1915	"	Battalion paraded at 1.15pm for Divine Service, Officers, C.S. Majors and Platoon Commanders attended a lecture given by the G.O.C. 1st Division at Bde Hd Qrs	

(73989) W4141—463. 400,000. 9/14. H.&J.Ltd. Forms/C. 2118/10.

Instructions regarding War Diaries and Intelligence Summaries are contained in F. S. Regs., Part II. and the Staff Manual respectively. Title pages will be prepared in manuscript.

WAR DIARY
or
~~INTELLIGENCE~~ SUMMARY.
(*Erase heading not required.*)

Army Form C. 2118.

Hour, Date, Place		Summary of Events and Information	Remarks and references to Appendices
15th February 1915	ECQUEDECQUES	2 Companies instruction in wire entanglements by R.E. 2 Companies routemarching	Capt C M H Massey and 102 other ranks joined
16th February 1915	"	2 Companies Rifle range 2 Companies practise the assault	
17th February 1915	"	2 Companies practise clearing obstacles. 2 companies entrenching.	
18th February 1915	"	Battalion route march	
19th February 1915	"	Battalion practise entrenching and advancing	
20th February 1915	"	2 Companies bathed at the Divisional Baths. 2 companies practised the assault	
21st February 1915	"	Battalion paraded for Divine Service at 1.45 pm	

164

(73989) W4141—463. 400,000. 9/14. H.&J.Ltd. Forms/C. 2118/10.

Army Form C. 2118.

Instructions regarding War Diaries and Intelligence Summaries are contained in F. S. Regs., Part II. and the Staff Manual respectively. Title pages will be prepared in manuscript.

WAR DIARY
or
~~INTELLIGENCE SUMMARY.~~

(Erase heading not required.)

Hour, Date, Place	Summary of Events and Information	Remarks and references to Appendices
22nd February 1915 ECQUEDECQUES.	Battalion Training	2/Lieut. H Johnstone joined
23rd February 1915 "	Battalion Training	
24th February 1915 "	Battalion Training	
25th February 1915 "	Battalion paraded at 11 30 am for inspection by G.O.C. 1st Corps.	
26th February 1915 "	Battalion Training. The advance and assault practised	
27th February 1915 " and billetted at HINGES	The Battalion left ECQUEDECQUES and marched to billets at HINGES	Capt EDH Tollemache 2 Lieut O.W.H. Leese, O. Campbell N.E.P. Sutton and 246 other ranks join.
28th February 1915 HINGES and billets at RICHEBOURG L'AVOUE'	The Battalion left HINGES and marched to billets at RICHEBOURG L'AVOUE'. In Brigade Reserve	1 6 E

(73989) W4141—463. 400,000. 9/14. H.&J.Ltd. Forms/C. 2118/10.

W A R   D I A R Y

1st COLDSTREAM GUARDS

March

1 9 1 5

Army Form C. 2118.

WAR DIARY
or
INTELLIGENCE SUMMARY.
(*Erase heading not required.*)

Instructions regarding War Diaries and Intelligence Summaries are contained in F. S. Regs., Part II. and the Staff Manual respectively. Title pages will be prepared in manuscript.

Hour, Date, Place	Summary of Events and Information	Remarks and references to Appendices
1st March 1915 RICHEBOURG L'AVOUE	In Brigade Reserve	
2nd March 1915 "	3 Companies went into the trenches and 1 company in reserve at Battn Head Qrs. relieved the Black Watch	16.1
3rd March 1915 "		Wounded Other ranks 3
4th March 1915 and billets at LE TOURET	Battalion relieved by the Black Watch and goes in billets at LE TOURET. In Brigade Reserve. Lt Col J Ponsonby resumed command of the Battalion from sick leave	Killed Other Ranks 2 Wounded Other Ranks 3
5th March 1915 LE TOURET	In Brigade Reserve.	20 Other ranks join from the Base
6th March 1915 LE TOURET and [illegible] at RICHEBOURG L'AVOUE	The Battalion relieved the Black Watch in the trenches 1 Company being in reserve at Battn Hd Qrs	
7th March 1915 RICHEBOURG L'AVOUE		

(73989) W4141—463. 400,000. 9/14. H.&J.Ltd. Forms/C. 2118/10.

Instructions regarding War Diaries and Intelligence Summaries are contained in F. S. Regs., Part II. and the Staff Manual respectively. Title pages will be prepared in manuscript.

Army Form C. 2118.

WAR DIARY
~~or~~
~~INTELLIGENCE SUMMARY.~~
(Erase heading not required.)

Hour, Date, Place	Summary of Events and Information	Remarks and references to Appendices
8th March 1915 RICHEBOURG L'AVOUE and billets at LE TOURET	Relieved by the Black Watch, go into Brigade Reserve at LE TOURET	Wounded Other Ranks: 2
9th March 1915 LE TOURET.	In Brigade Reserve	
10th March 1915 "	Battalion in billets in Brigade Reserve. Batt^n marched to RICHEBOURG ST VAAST	
11th March 1915 LE TOURET and trenches at RICHEBOURG L'AVOUE	Battalion relieved the Black Watch in the trenches at RICHEBOURG L'AVOUE	Killed: Other Ranks 1 Wounded: Other Ranks 5
12th March 1915 RICHEBOURG L'AVOUE		
13th March 1915 "		
14th March 1915 "	Relieved by the Black Watch and go into Brigade Reserve at LE TOURET.	
15 " " Billets in LE TOURET.		

(73989) W4141—463. 400,000. 9/14. H.&J.Ltd. Forms/C. 2118/10.

Instructions regarding War Diaries and Intelligence Summaries are contained in F. S. Regs., Part II. and the Staff Manual respectively. Title pages will be prepared in manuscript.

WAR DIARY
or
~~INTELLIGENCE~~ SUMMARY.

(*Erase heading not required.*)

Army Form C. 2118.

Hour, Date, Place		Summary of Events and Information	Remarks and references to Appendices
1915.			
March 16th.	LE TOURET. Batt. in billets.	The Battalion relieved 1st Black Watch in the trenches just S. of RUE du BOIS.	1, 6, 9
March 17th.	Trenches S. of RUE du BOIS.	A quiet day.	
March 18th.	Trenches S. of RUE du BOIS.	About midday the Germans shelled our second line heavily for an hour. This line was not held - so noone was hit. Relieved by 1st Black Watch about 7pm.	
March 19th.	Billets in LE TOURET.	Quiet day - weather cold & snow at night. A draft of 66 men joined the batt.	Lt. R. Beckwith Smith took over the adjutancy from Capt. W. R. Beckwith. Q.M.Sgt. Morris given a commission. [illegible] previously applied for him to return to Colchester.
March 20th.	Billets in LE TOURET.	Quiet day - more snow in the night. The Batt. relieved 1st Black Watch in the trenches.	
March 21st	Trenches S of RUE du BOIS.	Quiet day.	Capt. W. R. Beckwith appointed instructor at Bailleul military college.
March 22nd	Trenches S. of RUE du BOIS.	Quiet day. The Batt. is relieved by 1st Northamptons at 7pm & after relief marched to billets in Girls School in BETHUNE.	2/Lt. E. K. Stephenson granted 8 days leave. Sgt Baker No 1 Coy granted a commission.
March 23rd	Billets in BETHUNE.	The Battalion rested. 10% of the men only allowed leave at a time.	
March 24th.	Billets in BETHUNE.	At 4 pm the Battalion marched to billets at CORNET MALO. The billets were bad & much scattered about.	
March 25th	Billets at CORNET MALO.	About 5am a fire broke out in the Headquarter billets. One man (Pte Ligg) & a cow burned to death. O.R. Sgt Hammer, transport Sgt Thompson are detained in hospital with burnt hands.	
March 26th.	Billets at CORNET MALO.	Battalion resting. During this period of rest Coys do short route marches under Company arrangements.	Major J Steele joined the Batt. & took over duties of second in command.

(73989) W4141—463. 400,000. 9/14. H.&J.Ltd. Forms/C. 2118/10.

Army Form C. 2118.

Instructions regarding War Diaries and Intelligence Summaries are contained in F. S. Regs., Part II. and the Staff Manual respectively. Title pages will be prepared in manuscript.

WAR DIARY
~~or~~
~~INTELLIGENCE SUMMARY.~~

(*Erase heading not required.*)

Hour, Date, Place	Summary of Events and Information	Remarks and references to Appendices
March 27th Billets at CORNET MALO.	Battalion resting. Tubs were provided by the Brigade & every man was able to have a bath – the first for a month. Clean clothing also served out.	Capt. R.B.J. Crawford joined the Battn & took over command of No 2 Coy
March 28th Billets at CORNET MALO.	Battalion paraded for divine service in the open at 12 noon.	
March 29th Billets at CORNET MALO.	All bad boots in the battalion are changed at Divisional shoe-makers shop.	
March 30th Billets at CORNET MALO.	At 7.45 pm the Battalion moved to relieve the 5th Royal Sussex (2nd Brigade) in the trenches S. of RUE du BOIS in front of RICHEBOURG L'AVOUÉ. The relief is completed about 1am. Battn H.Q. on the CROIX BARBÉE – RICHEBOURG L'AVOUÉ road about 300 yards short of RUE du BOIS on the East side.	
March 31st Trenches S of RICHEBOURG L'AVOUÉ	Enemy's snipers extremely active – having evidently been allowed to do much as they liked for some time past. Here again the Battalion is in breastworks at a distance varying from 130 to 300 yards from the enemy. There is a very strong or ORCHARD KEEP occupied by our LEFT company & the left & centre coys are more in advance than the right. weather fine	
April 1st TRENCHES S of RICHEBOURG L'AVOUÉ.	Enemy's snipers again active & it was almost impossible to put show your head in the front trench for more than a second without being hit. weather fine.	Captn Massey wounded in the leg.
April 2nd TRENCHES S. of RICHEBOURG L'AVOUÉ	A quieter day. "A" coy 21st London Regiment is attached to Battn for instruction – one platoon to each company. This company was handed over to 1st Bn Scots Guards	Capt R.B.J. Crawford went sick with a strained ankle.
April 3rd " "	A short bombardment with artillery machine guns & rifle fire ordered at 4.30 am. The Germans opened rapid fire at 4.25 am. The Battalion is rather worried all day by the enemy's light field or P.P. Squeak gun. At 7.30 pm the Battalion is relieved by 1st SCOTS GUARDS & marched to billets – right half Battalion & H.Q. to LE TOURET Left half Battn under Major J Steele to RICHEBOURG ST VAAST.	Lt. D. M. B. Hall was knocked down by a shell & reported wounded, having but his shoulder out.

(73989) W4141—463. 400,000. 9/14. H.&J.Ltd. Forms/C. 2118/10.

1st Infantry Brigade.

1st Division.

WAR DIARY

1st COLDSTREAM GUARDS.

APRIL

1915

On His Majesty's Service.

Copy. WAR DIARY

Date	Place	Entry	Remarks
April 1st	Trenches S. of RICHEBOURG L'AVOUE	Enemy's snipers again active & it is almost impossible to show your head in the front trench for more than a second without being hit. Weather fine	Capt C. Massey wounded in the leg.
April 2nd	do. do.	A quieter day "A" Coy 21st London Regt. is attached to Battn. for instruction – one platoon to each Company. This Company was handed over to 1st Bn Scots Guards.	Capt R.B.T. Crawfurd went sick with a strained ankle
April 3rd	" "	A short bombardment with artillery, machine gun & rifle fire ordered at 4.30 am. The Germans opened rapid fire at 4.25 AM The Battn is rather worried all day by the enemy's light field or Pip-Squeak gun. At 7.30 pm the Battn is relieved by 1st Scots Guards & marched to billets – right half Battn & HQ to LE TOURET – left half Bn under Major J. Steele to RICHEBOURG St. VAAST.	Lt. D.M.B. Hull was knocked down by a shell & reported wounded having put his shoulder out.

Instructions regarding War Diaries and Intelligence Summaries are contained in F. S. Regs., Part II. and the Staff Manual respectively. Title pages will be prepared in manuscript.

WAR DIARY
or
~~INTELLIGENCE SUMMARY.~~

(*Erase heading not required.*)

Army Form C. 2118.

Hour, Date, Place	Summary of Events and Information	Remarks and references to Appendices
April 3rd (cont) Trenches S. of RICHEBOURG L'AVOUÉ	During the period March 31st - April 3rd the Battalion suffered the following casualties:- 2 officers wounded, 7 other ranks killed, 6 " " wounded.	
April 4th Billets at LE TOURET & RICHEBOURG ST VAAST.	Battalion resting	
April 5th, April 6th, April 7th Billets at LE TOURET / RICHEBOURG ST VAAST	Battalion resting. On april 6th a few big shells fell near the billets of the left half battalion, forcing them to take to their dug outs for an hour. On april 7th at about 7pm the battalion relieved the 1st Cameron Highlanders in the trenches, just on the right or S.W. of their last position in the trenches.	
April 8th Trenches S. of RICHEBOURG L'AVOUÉ	The Battalion is again in breastworks. The main line running parallel with the RUE du BOIS & about 100 yards S. of it from the point where the RUE du BOIS & the QUINQUE RUE roads meet in a N.E. direction for about 600 yards. Battn H.Q. were in a comfortable house in RUE des BERCEAUX. There were a line of Butts in front but these were gradually joined up with a view to their eventually becoming the front & main line of defence. "C" coy 21st London regiment handed over by Camerons & used as a company.	
April 9th " "	A quiet day. [The weather became stormy & cold. At 9.30 pm there was a false alarm of a German attack impending. The Battalion & all the neighbouring batteries stood to arms for about an hour.	

(73989) W4141—463. 400,000. 9/14. H.&J.Ltd. Forms/C. 2118/10.

Instructions regarding War Diaries and Intelligence Summaries are contained in F. S. Regs., Part II. and the Staff Manual respectively. Title pages will be prepared in manuscript.

WAR DIARY
~~or~~
~~INTELLIGENCE SUMMARY.~~

(*Erase heading not required.*)

Army Form C. 2118.

Hour, Date, Place	Summary of Events and Information	Remarks and references to Appendices
April 10th. Trenches S of RICHEBOURG L'AVOUÉ	A quiet day. A draft of 125 men joined the Battalion. 1 Coy 21st London relieved withdrawn.	Lt. R. J. M. Riley joined Battn. - Posted to No. ... 2t Lt D Browne took over command of No 4 Coy.
April 11th " "	A quiet day & quite hot weather. "A" Coy 23rd Battalion is attached to Battn for instructional purposes - one platoon to each company. The Brigade H.Q. seemed to expect an attack.	Gen. C. Pole-Carew visited Battn. H.Q.
April 12th " "	A quiet day. Officers patrols reconnoitred the German wire.	
April 13th " "	A quiet day. Fresh orders for defence of our section were issued entailing a large amount of work on the front or Bust line.	
April 14th " "	About 4 pm Germans shelled Albert road just behind our line with Black Marias - no damage done. Draft of 29 men joined Battn. Fighting strength 884	
April 15 " "	Rue du BOIS heavily shelled by [illegible] squeak guns about 12 noon otherwise a quiet day. The Battn was relieved about 8 pm by the South Wales Borderers of the 3rd Brigade. On completion of relief the Battn marched back to the same billets as before in CORNET MALO. Two men killed during this period in the trenches	Coy Sgt Major Goldsmith granted a commission in the 2nd Bn Royal Welsh Fusiliers.
April 16th. Billets at CORNET MALO	The Battalion rested.	
April 17th.	Short route march executed by coys. Lecture to all officers & platoon commanders by Major General Haking in LOCON at 5 pm.	

Instructions regarding War Diaries and Intelligence Summaries are contained in F. S. Regs., Part II. and the Staff Manual respectively. Title pages will be prepared in manuscript.

WAR DIARY
or
~~INTELLIGENCE~~ SUMMARY.
(*Erase heading not required.*)

Army Form C. 2118.

Hour, Date, Place	Summary of Events and Information	Remarks and references to Appendices
April 18th Billets in CORNET MALO	Church parade at 10.30 am. Bn parade 1.30 pm for training in BOIS du PACAULT. The weather has become much warmer.	
April 19th " "	Instruction of N.C.O.s carried out. Bn came into waiting at 6 pm.	
April 20th " "	Battn in waiting up till 6 pm. Battn paraded at 9.30 am for inspection by C.O. Points noticed:- Lack of cap stars - hair too long - boots too big.	Major Hon C. Willoughby went sick to BETHUNE
April 21st " "	Bn paraded at 8.30 am for training in BOIS du PACAULT.	Capt E. D. H. Tollemache, Lt. Hon Wm H. D. Browne, 2nd Lt. T. A. Tapp, 2nd Lt. W. S. B. Bosanquet } Leave to England. 21.4.15 to 27.4.15.
April 22nd " "	Companies at disposal of O.C. companies.	
April 23rd " "	Battn practised getting out of a breastwork & over a ditch & wire & charging another breastwork. The whole Battn left billets at 5.15 pm for a fatigue behind RICHEBOURG L'AVOUÉ - digging narrow trenches for telephone wires & filling these in. The Battn did not get back to billets till 2.30 am 24.4.15	
April 24th " " to billets in OBLINGHEM	The Battn left CORNET MALO at 5.15 pm & marched to new billets in OBLINGHEM.	
April 25th Billets in OBLINGHEM	The Battn is in waiting. The Brigade formed Corps Reserve. Church parade cancelled owing to person being ill.	

Instructions regarding War Diaries and Intelligence Summaries are contained in F. S. Regs., Part II. and the Staff Manual respectively. Title pages will be prepared in manuscript.

WAR DIARY
or
INTELLIGENCE SUMMARY.
(Erase heading not required.)

Army Form C. 2118.

Hour, Date, Place	Summary of Events and Information	Remarks and references to Appendices
April 26th Billets in OBLINGHEM.	The Battn paraded at 9.10 am & marched to a point near CORNET MALO, where they practised attacking out of a breastwork, getting over a stream & through gaps in the enemys wire. Sir James Willcox, Gen Munro & many other generals came to watch the proceedings.	Lt. J. the Younger joined Battn. Posted to 2o 2 Coy.
April 27th Billets in OBLINGHEM	The court of Inquiry on all men missing over 6 months started on this day	Capt R. B. J. Crawfurd accidentally wounded by a bomb – went to Hosp 28-4-15.
April 28th " "	Coys practised the attack in conjunction with machine guns. Weather very hot.	Lts Hon J. Browne, W. S. B. Bosanquet & T. A. Tapp rejoined from leave – Capt S. D. Tollemache did not return having been appointed G.S.O. 3 to Lowland Divn.
April 29th " "	Coys went for short route march	
April 30th " "	Coys went for short route march – All corporals paraded for practise in handling sections.	Lt. Hon. J. Browne, Lt W. S. B. Bosanquet } admitted to hospital.

1st Infantry Brigade.

1st Division.

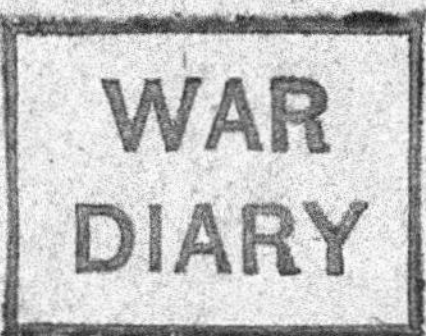

1st COLDSTREAM GUARDS.

M A Y

1 9 1 5

Brigade Operation
Orders.

1st Coldstream Guards.

May 1915.

May 1st.	"	[Coys for route march. Corporals paraded again.] A draft of 25 men under	Major A. ? Egerton joined the Battalion.
May 2nd.	"	Church parade at 11 am. Bn. paraded at 5.10pm & marched via LOCON - LACOUTURE - RICHEBOURG St VAAST to relieve the Northamptons in dug outs & billets about cross roads (WINDY CORNER) half a mile N of RICHEBOURG L'AVOUÉ. Relief completed by 10pm. H.Q. at WINDY CORNER in a very bad & dirty place.	

(73989) W4141—463. 400,000. 9/14. H.&J.Ltd. Forms/C. 2118/10.

Instructions regarding War Diaries and Intelligence Summaries are contained in F. S. Regs., Part II. and the Staff Manual respectively. Title pages will be prepared in manuscript.

WAR DIARY
or
INTELLIGENCE SUMMARY.
(Erase heading not required.)

Army Form C. 2118.

Hour, Date, Place	Summary of Events and Information	Remarks and references to Appendices
May 3rd Billets + dug outs ~~N of~~ RICHEBOURG L'AVOUÉ.	Fresh batteries were brought up near H.Q. of the Battn. A hot but quiet day.	
May 4th ..	A heavy thunderstorm came on about 5 pm. The Prince of Wales was coming to see the Battn. but did not turn up.) The Battn was relieved by London Scottish about 8 pm + then in turn relieved the Scots Guards in the front 2 lines. Nos 1 + 2 Coys in the front line - Nos 3 + 4 in support.	
May 5th Breastworks S. of RICHEBOURG L'AVOUÉ	Enemy's snipers active. RUE DU BOIS shelled in afternoon by 6 inch howitzers.	
May 6th ..	Shelling very heavy on both sides our guns registering - orders received. Shift into Bn H.Q.	
May 7th ..	Shelling again v. heavy further orders for the attack issued. All coy commanders went into Ritz (artillery observation Station) to look at the ground. At the last moment - about 7 pm - operations are postponed - the Battn is not relieved -	
May 8th ..	A quiet day the guns all having registered. Further preparations for the attack but not till) pm did we hear for certain that operations were to be carried out. The Bn was relieved by the Munsters + Welch Regiment. Owing to congested state of the roads relief was not completed till 12 mn. The Battn then bivouaced in + around COMPTON FARM about 800 yards S.W. of church in RICHEBOURG ST VAAST.	

(73989) W4141—463. 400,000. 9/14. H.&J.Ltd. Forms/C. 2118/10.

Instructions regarding War Diaries and Intelligence Summaries are contained in F. S. Regs., Part II. and the Staff Manual respectively. Title pages will be prepared in manuscript.

WAR DIARY
or
INTELLIGENCE SUMMARY.
(*Erase heading not required.*)

Army Form C. 2118.

Hour, Date, Place	Summary of Events and Information	Remarks and references to Appendices
May 9th Operations at RUE du BOIS	at 3.30 am the Battn stood to arms - & at 5am moved under any available cover close at hand. The guns had started shooting at about 4.30am tho' the bombardment did not really begin till 5am, the assault being timed for 5.40 am. At 6.30am the Battn moved by companies up the ALBERT ROAD into C line of breastworks immediately N of the RUE du BOIS between ALBERT & EDWARD ROADS. Battn H.Q. remained about the centre until 3pm when they moved 200 yards further W. On arrival in C line information was received that the assault had failed - & that another was to be attempted at 12 noon. This was postponed till 3.40 pm - when 2 battns of the 1st Brigade (The Black Watch & 1st Camerons) were detailed to deliver it in the place of 2 battns of the 2nd Brigade - which by that time were much shattered both by the failure of the 1st assault & by subsequent shell fire - which was very heavy in the front two lines. The remainder of the 1st Brigade remained in support - the 1st Coldstream on the right with 3 coys in C line & ~~one~~ coy in D line. The London Scottish were on our left & the Scots Guards beyond on their left. Owing to the blocking of the communication trench the Camerons were 45 minutes late. The Black Watch went on alone & about 50 men succeeded in reaching & occupying the 1st German breastwork - but being unsupported they were subsequently bombed out. After the failure of the second assault the Battn was detailed to remain in support throughout the night but this order was cancelled [illegible] Battn marched by coys to billets [illegible] HINGES.	

Instructions regarding War Diaries and Intelligence Summaries are contained in F. S. Regs., Part II. and the Staff Manual respectively. Title pages will be prepared in manuscript.

WAR DIARY
or
INTELLIGENCE SUMMARY.
(*Erase heading not required.*)

Army Form C. 2118.

Hour, Date, Place	Summary of Events and Information	Remarks and references to Appendices
May 9th Operations at RUE du BOIS (cont)	The last company did not reach HINGES until 6.30am on the 10th. Throughout the 9th the Battn was under heavy shell fire - which added to the noise of our own guns was extremely trying. The Battn was protected to a great extent by the houses of the RUE du BOIS as well as the breastworks specially built. It is probably owing to the former that our losses were so comparatively small amounting as they did to 1 killed - 16 wounded + 5 missing. Sgt Buck - machine gun sgt - who had been through the whole campaign + had been awarded the D.C.M. - was the only man to be killed.	Lt. Hon. T. Agar Robartes was wounded v. slightly in the arm finger + leg but remained at duty.
May 10th Billets in HINGES	The Battn rested.	
" 11th " " "	" " "	
May 12th Billets in HINGES	At 10.25 am Battn paraded - halted for dinners near BETHUNE + afterwards marched on to LE PREOL where the battn was in brigade reserve. All 3 Battns of the COLDSTREAM met in this village - the 1st Brigade took over from the 4th Brigade.	2nd Lt. O. Styles No 1 Coy, 2nd Lt. R.P. Pearse No 2 Coy, 2nd Lt. C.W.D Parish No 3 Coy } Joined the Battn.
[illegible] Billets in LE PREOL.	A wet day. At 4pm notice was received that the Brigade would probably be relieved. It was, by territorials (London) + at 9pm marched by canal bank to billets in RUE d'AIRE BETHUNE arriving about 11.40pm. BETHUNE was shelled	Capt. E. Jarrett No 3 Coy, " R. Feilding No 4 } Joined the Battn from 3rd R[illegible]

(73989) W4141—463. 400,000. 9/14. H.&J.Ltd. Forms/C. 2118/10.

Instructions regarding War Diaries and Intelligence Summaries are contained in F. S. Regs., Part II. and the Staff Manual respectively. Title pages will be prepared in manuscript.

WAR DIARY
or
INTELLIGENCE SUMMARY.
(Erase heading not required.)

Army Form C. 2118.

Hour, Date, Place	Summary of Events and Information	Remarks and references to Appendices
May 14th Billets in BETHUNE	Battn rested in billets in RUE D'AIRE. A draft of 30 other ranks under 2 Lt R.T. Burton joined the Battn.	2 Lt. R.T. Burton joined Battn.
May 15th " "	At 2.15 pm the Battn paraded & marched to billets in SAILLY LABOURSE & VERMELLES. [Nos 1 & 2 Coys & 2 machine guns were billeted at the latter place under Major J Steele. The remainder of the battalion were in the chateau at SAILLY LABOURSE] These were the best billets that the battalion had been in since the beginning of the war. They had previously been occupied by by the French, whom the remainder of the brigade relieved in the front line of trenches. The Battn is in brigade reserve. Operation orders attached.	
May 16th Billets at SAILLY LABOURSE	Voluntary service at 7.30am & 6pm. The Division was now a part of what was known as "Barters Force". Heavy firing all day on our left, where 7th & 2nd Divisions were attacking.	
May 17th " "	Weather became very wet. There was heavy firing to the N.E. all the night of the 16-17th May. News received during the morning that 2nd & 7th Divisions have taken some trenches in front of PRINCES ROAD - the 2nd Division meeting with the most opposition - that they must be out of at 10.30pm the Battn received orders	

Instructions regarding War Diaries and Intelligence Summaries are contained in F. S. Regs., Part II. and the Staff Manual respectively. Title pages will be prepared in manuscript.

WAR DIARY
or
INTELLIGENCE SUMMARY.
(Erase heading not required.)

Army Form C. 2118.

Hour, Date, Place	Summary of Events and Information	Remarks and references to Appendices
May 17th Billets in SAILLY LABOURSE	the billets they were then occupying by 9.30 am as they were to be used as Divisional Hdqrs.	2nd Lt C. E. Green went to hospital "sick"
May 18th Billets in SAILLY LABOURSE	At 9 am No 4 Coy (2 platoons) moved into new billets in the village 2 platoons remaining where they were. No 3 moved at 9.15 am to the western part of the village & H.Qrs at 9.30 am to a house 100 yards west of the shrine. All the billets were dirty - previously having been occupied by the French troops. Weather very wet. [illegible] Battn had to find working parties of 150 men.	
May 19th	The 2 Coys at VERMELLES relieved the 2 coys of the [illegible] Scots Guards in the front trenches of Y.1. beginning at 6 pm. The relief had to be done down 1½ miles of communication trench & was completed before dark. Nos 3 & 4 Coys marched from billets in SAILLY LABOURSE by platoons beginning at 7.30 pm. Hdqrs did not move till 8.30 pm. As it was dark when coys arrived at VERMELLES the road up to new Battn H.Q. (at LE RUTOIRE) was used. No 3 Coy was in a support trench - No 4 Coy in dug outs near Battn H.Q. Battn H.Q were for the most part in cellars in the farm at LE RUTOIRE. The C.O had a wonderful dug out made by the French. It resembled the "Tube" in shape & was lined with iron plates. The Trenches & dug outs were all in a very dirty	

(73989) W4141—463. 400,000. 9/14. H.&J.Ltd. Forms/C. 2118/10.

16a

Instructions regarding War Diaries and Intelligence Summaries are contained in F. S. Regs., Part II. and the Staff Manual respectively. Title pages will be prepared in manuscript.

WAR DIARY
or
INTELLIGENCE SUMMARY.
(Erase heading not required.)

Army Form C. 2118.

Hour, Date, Place	Summary of Events and Information	Remarks and references to Appendices
	state, as the Scots Guards had taken them over from the French & had not had time to thoroughly clean the lines up. The London Scottish (2 coys) were on our left & the French on our right. The front trench was almost semicircular & was not completed to join up with the French on the right - tho the coys in support were in touch with them. The German trenches were about 1000 yards off - they were able to enfilade almost all the front trench from two sides. The remainder of the trenches & dug outs were good - the line was well wired. The country was very open all round.	
May 20th Trenches near LE RHTOIRE.	Enemy shelled our left front coy (No 2 Coy) with some heavy shells during the afternoon - getting a direct hit on a dug out & killing two N.C.O.s. From 10.30pm to 12 mn the machine guns were ordered to open short bursts of rapid fire on German advanced works. During the night the right of the front trench was extended about 50 yards towards the French.	Other Ranks 2 Killed } No. 9157 Sgt Coleman, No. 6250 Pte Norton 1 wounded

(73989) W4141—463. 400,000. 9/14. H.&J.Ltd. Forms/C. 2118/10.

Instructions regarding War Diaries and Intelligence Summaries are contained in F. S. Regs., Part II. and the Staff Manual respectively. Title pages will be prepared in manuscript.

WAR DIARY
or
INTELLIGENCE SUMMARY.
(*Erase heading not required.*)

Army Form C. 2118.

Hour, Date, Place	Summary of Events and Information	Remarks and references to Appendices
May 21st. Trenches E. of LE RUTOIRE	Enemy's guns again active but no damage done. The coys in the front line were somewhat worried during the night by enfilade machine gun fire from the S.E. The gun was thought to be located on the VERMELLES - HULLOCH road. Nos 3 & 4 Coys relieved Nos 2 & 1 Coys respectively in the front line of trenches about 6 pm. There was a scare about midnight that Battns on our left were standing to arms. This proved to be incorrect. Heavy firing during night 21st - 22nd round to the N.	Major Steele left Battn to see his brother (? 1st Royal Dragoons) who had been severely wounded at Ypres & was in hosp at BAILLEUL. (Col Steele died of his wounds 22.5.15)
May 22nd. " "	A very hot day. Enemy guns less active. 117th Battery in support worked on principle of 2 shells to German one. 43rd [?] Batt. came into position & otherwise no guns in support of us. There was a very heavy thunderstorm during the night 22-23rd & also tremendous firing to the South.	
May 23rd. " "	A few heavy shells & high explosives dropped near Battn H.Q. but no damage done. Nos 3 & 4 Coys were relieved at 6 pm by	

Instructions regarding War Diaries and Intelligence Summaries are contained in F. S. Regs., Part II. and the Staff Manual respectively. Title pages will be prepared in manuscript.

WAR DIARY
or
INTELLIGENCE SUMMARY.
(Erase heading not required.)

Army Form C. 2118.

Hour, Date, Place	Summary of Events and Information	Remarks and references to Appendices
May 23rd (cont)	2 Coys of the 1st Scots Guards. This relief was successfully completed by 7.30pm. The remainder of the Battn were relieved at 9.30pm. The whole Battn was in billets at SAILLY LABOURSE by 12.30am. H.Q. Nos 3 & 4 Coys were billeted as before – nos 1 & 2 Coys being billeted towards the eastern end of the village.	Major Steele returned to Battn.
May 24th Billets in SAILLY LABOURSE	At 2 pm H.Q. & Nos 3 & 4 Coys moved their billets to the eastern end of the village so that the whole Battn should be together. H.Q. were in a house near the church. The weather had now become very hot. News was received that Italy had declared war. (It was also rumoured that the Battn was to attack the triangle at CUINCHY, or Brickstacks, and the Coldstream were longing to get some of their own back.) 2 Coys of the Black Watch moved from SAILLY LABOURSE up to NOYELLES LEZ-VERMELLES	Major J. Steele left at 5pm to take over command of the 2nd Bn.
May 25th	all coys employed in cleaning up the billets & streets which were in filthy condition. During this period in SAILLY LABOURSE the Battn had to find a working party of [illegible] & 50 men to work under the sanitary authorities morning & afternoon.	
May 26th	Coys went for a short route march of about 6 miles. weather very hot.	

(73989) W4141—463. 400,000. 9/14. H.&J.Ltd. Forms/C. 2118/10.

Instructions regarding War Diaries and Intelligence Summaries are contained in F. S. Regs., Part II. and the Staff Manual respectively. Title pages will be prepared in manuscript.

WAR DIARY
or
INTELLIGENCE SUMMARY.
(Erase heading not required.)

Army Form C. 2118.

Hour, Date, Place	Summary of Events and Information	Remarks and references to Appendices
May 27th. Billets in SAILLY LABOURSE	Enemy dropped a few shells round the village but no damage done. At 4.30 pm Nos 3 & 4 Coys moved off to relieve the 2 Coys of the Scots Guards in the front trenches of Y1. This relief was completed before dark. The reliefs were shelled & 2 men wounded. The remainder of the Battn left billets between 7.30 & 8.30 pm & the whole relief was completed by 11.30 pm. The Scots Guards had done a lot of work & the front trench had been joined up with the French. weather cooler.	
May 28th. Trenches East of LE RUTOIRE (near VERMELLES)	One man killed in the early morning by a sniper - thought to be at close range. In the afternoon 2 enemy aeroplanes seen - & driven off by anti-aircraft guns. Enemy shelled C.T. just behind Bn H.Q. & cut the telephone wire. weather warmer.	
May 29th. " "	A quiet day. Enemy always more active in the evening & seem to shell communication trenches then. another hostile aeroplane seen. about 11.15 pm & 12 mn 2 patrols went out to the "Lone Tree" about 400 yards in front of our lines. The first under 2/Lt C. Sutton was challenged in German & managed to get away - the second was challenged in	

(73989) W4141—463. 400,000. 9/14. H.&J.Ltd. Forms/C. 2118/10.

Instructions regarding War Diaries and Intelligence Summaries are contained in F. S. Regs., Part II. and the Staff Manual respectively. Title pages will be prepared in manuscript.

WAR DIARY
or
INTELLIGENCE SUMMARY.
(*Erase heading not required.*)

Army Form C. 2118.

Hour, Date, Place	Summary of Events and Information	Remarks and references to Appendices
	English so the patrol thinking their own snipers were in front of them walked on. They were fired on at point blank range & One man was reported to be killed – & was left behind but the rest (3) managed to get away – one of these being wounded. Later during the night a sniper missed his way & must have been taken prisoner as he was never seen again.	
May 30th Trenches East of LE RUTOIRE	a quiet day except for a few small shells which fell just behind Bn. H.Q between 5 & 6 pm.	2/Lt R Peake joined the Battn
May 31st	at 10 am orders received that Battn would not be relieved till night of June 1st – 2nd by 140th Brigade. The remainder of the day was quiet.	

BRIGADE OPERATION ORDERS.

Copy No. 2

Operation Order No.5
by
Brigadier-General, H.C.Lowther, C.V.O., C.M.G., D.S.O.
Commanding 1st Guards Brigade.

BETHUNE.
15th May 1915.

Reference BETHUNE Map.
1/40,000

1. The Brigade will march to-day as follows, to relieve 58th French Division in Section Y (3rd Brigade have taken over Section Z on our left

(a). 1st Coldstream Guards at 2.15 p.m. to billets in SAILLY LABOURSE.
1st Black Watch at 4.30 p.m. to billets in SAILLY LABOURSE.
1st Scots Guards at 5 p.m. to relieve the right of the French Y.1
London Scottish at 5.15 p.m. to relieve the centre of the French Y.2
1st Cameron Highlanders at 6.30 p.m. (to march behind London Scottish) to relieve the left of the French in Y.3

(b). East of the cross roads in L.4c.5.8 Battalions will march in small parties at intervals of 200 yards on each side of the road during daylight. Carts will go down singly.

2.(a) On arrival at SAILLY LABOURSE the 1st Coldstream Guards will at once send 2 companies to VERMELLES. These companies will be marched up in parties of not more than 10 men, and at intervals of 200 yards. Each party to go direct to it's billets and remain in them till the relief is completed.

(b). They will take 5 S.A.A.Carts with them, and dump the ammunition at Bde ~~Headquarters~~ Advanced Reporting Centre (G.8.a.5.2). Carts to go up at intervals of ½ mile and return singly to SAILLY LABOURSE immediately they have dumped the ammunition.

(c). This ammunition will be Brigade Reserve, and the ½ Battalion in Brigade Reserve at VERMELLES will find a guard over this.

3. The three Battalions going into the trenches will take up their 8 S.A.A.Carts, dump the ammunition and then send the carts back to SAILLY LABOURSE.

4. 1st Line Transport will march immediately in rear of units, and will all be billeted at SAILLY LABOURSE.

5. The Lowland Field Company R.E. is allotted to Y Section and will be billeted in SAILLY LABOURSE.

6. No.3 Field Ambulance will form an Aid Post in VERMELLES.

7. No.2 Coy.Train and baggage Section will be at FOUQUIERES LEZ BETHUNE E.21.a.5.7.

8. Brigade Headquarters will be in NOYELLES LEZ VERMELLES L.11.b.8.

9. 1st Coldstream Guards will find a Control Post at cross roads L.11.c.9.5. Orders for Control Posts attached.

R. K. Brooke
Major,
Brigade Major, 1st Guards Brigade.

Copy No.1 Office.
Copies Nos. 2 to Coldstream, 3 to Scots Gds, 4 to Black Watch, 5 to Camerons, 6 to London Scottish, 7 to No.2 Coy Train.

Coldstream Gds

* * * * * * * * * * * * * * * * * *

The following notes on necessary work in the trenches are circulated to all Battalions in order that they may know what to carry on with as soon as they take over.

1. Work which entails a shovel showing over the parapet is to be avoided by day as it always draws shell-fire.
R.E. help will rarely be available; when available for special work Commanding Officers will be informed.

2. <u>All Sections.</u> Sanitation. Covering of existing old latrine-places. Establishment of biscuit tin latrines. ~~Maintainenance~~ Maintenance of wire in front by repairing places where it has been cut by our own bullets or in preparation for a French attack. Sufficient ~~exists~~ exits for patrols must be left.
Adaption of <u>all</u> machine-gun emplacements for use with our guns.
Maintenance of trenches and dug-outs. The wood-work of the latter is not to be ~~moved~~ removed even though we are not occupying them, other people may need them.
Establishment of bomb depots in and near front line.

3. <u>Y.1</u> Completion of new front trench and wiring same. Wire to be placed in continuation of it to the right. Deepening of communication trench on left of new front trench.

4. <u>Y.2.</u> Construction of new communication trench on line of that already begun by the French.

5. In every section a minimum reserve of 16 boxes S.A.A. per Company in front or second line is to be maintained.

6. <u>Brigade.S.A.A.Reserve Depot. G.7.b.7.4.</u> *9*
This Depot will be in charge of the 2 Companies of Brigade Reserve in VERMELLES.

VERY Lights.	Can be drawn from *there* by units in the front line.	
Rifle Grenades.		

Tools. 300 shovels.
150 picks.

Battalions must return tools to this Depot, as soon as they have finished with them.

7. <u>R.E. Store at</u> *VERMELLES.*

Bombs.	Can be drawn direct by Battalions from this store.
Sandbags.	
Barbed wire.	

8. <u>Traffic Regulations etc for VERMELLES.</u>
(a). The ½ Battalion in Brigade Reserve at VERMELLES will establish Control Posts on all the roads leading out of VERMELLES with the exception of the road immediately south of the Church. The Battalion holding Y.2 will be responsible for this road.
The Posts will see that men do not collect in the streets but remain under cover.
(b). All wheeled transport by day and night will use the track through L.11.b and L.12.a. This is not shown on the map.
(c). Wheeled transport is not to go into VERMELLES by day except under exceptional circumstances and both by day and night vehicles are to move singly.
(d). Supplies, cookers, water carts etc going up at night will go up and return singly.

[signature] Major,

16/5/15. Brigade Major, 1st Guards Brigade.

Copy of para 8 has been sent to your Q.M.

. Bolds. Gds. . .

1. (a). On 27th May the Coldstream Guards will relieve the Scots Guards in Sub-Section Y.1 using the road L.11.d, L.18.a and G.13.b. The 2 front companies will be relieved by day. Guides to meet these companies at 6 p.m. at junction of C.T.58 and C.T.60

The Black Watch will relieve the Camerons in Sub-Section Y.3 using the road L.11.b andL.12.a.

London Scottish will remain in Y.2.

(b). If it is desired 2 Companies Black Watch now in VERMELLES may relieve 2 Companies Camerons by day.

(c). No other troops to move east of fork roads in L.3.b.6.4 before 7.30 p.m.

2. On relief Camerons will take over the billets of Coldstream Guards in SAILLY LABOURSE.

Scots Guards the billets of Black Watch in VERMELLES and NOYELLES LES VERMELLES. These Battalions will be in Brigade Reserve.

3. Machine Guns.

London Scottish will return the two machine guns to Black Watch to-morrow night and will take over two from the Camerons.

~~Scots Guards will hand over one machine gun to Coldstream Guards.~~

4. Attention is called to Orders for Brigade Reserve. O.C., Companies in VERMELLES will report to O.Cs, Y.1 and Y.3 respectively, and will be responsible for the maintenance, and cleaning of C.T.60 and Central C.T. respectively.

5. The Scots Guards will take over the Brigade S.A.A. Reserve Depot G.7.b.9.4. The Brigade Reserve of 300 Shovels and 150 picks or a receipt of the unit in possession of the tools will be taken over.

6. Ammunition, Bombs, VERY Lights, Vermorel Sprayers, etc, are to be handed over. C.Os will arrange to take over the Mobilization tools from Battalions in the trenches, and hand over an equivalent number from their tool carts in SAILLY LABOURSE.

7. The Camerons will take over the Control Post at L.3.b.6.4 from Coldstream Guards at 7 p.m. to-morrow.

8. Details of relief will be arranged by Officers Commanding Battalions.

9. O.C., Relieving Battalions will report this as soon as the relief is completed.

R. B. Bruce [signature]

Major,

26/5/15. Brigade Major, 1st Guards Brigade.

1st Infantry Brigade.

1st Division.

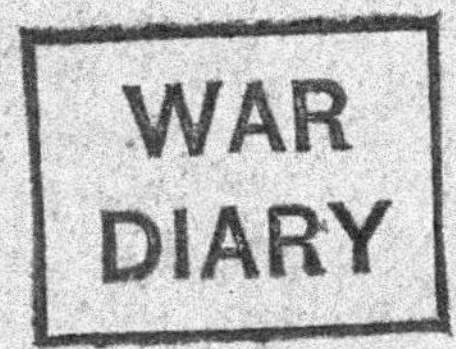

1st COLDSTREAM GUARDS.

JUNE

1915

Appendices.

On His Majesty's Service.

1st Coldstream Guards.

June 1915.

June 1st " " "	a Danish General + A.D.C. came round the trenches about 3 pm. about 5.30 pm the enemy shelled VERMELLES very heavily with 6" howitzers – searching for a battery in position behind the wall of the mine. Fortunately all but 2 sections of the battery had been removed + no damage was done	1 O.R. Killed.

(73989) W4141—463. 400,000. 9/14. H.&J.Ltd. Forms/C. 2118/10. at about 10pm the first relief of the 7th London Regiment

Instructions regarding War Diaries and Intelligence Summaries are contained in F. S. Regs., Part II. and the Staff Manual respectively. Title pages will be prepared in manuscript.

WAR DIARY
or
INTELLIGENCE SUMMARY.
(*Erase heading not required.*)

Army Form C. 2118.

Hour, Date, Place	Summary of Events and Information	Remarks and references to Appendices
	began to arrive. The relief was completed by 1 am & Coys marched independently to billets in the Tobacco factory in BETHUNE. all coys being in billets by 3.45 am.	
June 2nd Billets in BETHUNE. (Tobacco Factory)	Precautions had to be taken about protection from shell fire as the town had been shelled daily for some time past. In case of heavy shelling the Battn was ordered to go to the PRIEURE St PRY about 2 miles S.W. of the town.	
June 3rd " " " King's Birthday.	a telegram (attached) was sent to H.M. the King from all 3 Battns of the Regiment addressed to the Private Secretary: "The three Battns Coldstream Guards in France wish your Majesty many congratulations today." Three coys bathed in the bath in the Boulevard THIERS	
June 4th	Two coys again bathed in the baths in the Boulevard THIERS all old Etonian officers celebrated the 4th June by a dinner at Battn H.Q. about 20 officers were present 12 of these belonging to the Coldstream. a telegram (attached) was received from the King by all three Battns	

Instructions regarding War Diaries and Intelligence Summaries are contained in F. S. Regs., Part II. and the Staff Manual respectively. Title pages will be prepared in manuscript.

WAR DIARY
or
INTELLIGENCE SUMMARY.
(*Erase heading not required.*)

Army Form C. 2118.

Hour, Date, Place	Summary of Events and Information	Remarks and references to Appendices
June 4th (cont) Billets in BETHUNE.	Following from the King: "The message which I have received from the three Battalions of my Coldstream Guards at the Front on the anniversary of my birthday has greatly touched me aaa Please convey to all ranks my warmest thanks for their congratulations + good wishes & tell them how proud I am of their achievements"	2Lt. W. Johnston leave to England.
	The question of an attack on the trenches in front of CUINCHY was discussed & the B? orders	ready by the 8th inst
June 5th Billets in BETHUNE.	The Battn paraded at 9.30 am in marching order for inspection by the G.O.C. 1st Corps (Monro) & 1st Division (Haking), who arrived at 10 am. Two coys were drawn up inside the yard of the Tobacco factory + two outside in the street. Both Generals were much pleased with the appearance of the Battn on parade & stated that they were as fine a body of men as they had ever seen.	2Lts C.E. Green & [illegible] (both Special reservists) were granted permanent commissions in the Coldstream about this time.
	A draft of 50 N.C.O's & men joined the Battn at 6pm under [illegible]	2Lt J.R. Woods joined Bn.
	The enemy dropped a few shells on the town about 400 yards up the street (west) wounding 2 men &	Lt R.T. Burton wounded.
June 6th	The C.O. & O.C. coys went up to see the trenches in front of CUINCHY.	
	Bad news, the fall of PRZEMYSL is received.	

Instructions regarding War Diaries and Intelligence Summaries are contained in F. S. Regs., Part II. and the Staff Manual respectively. Title pages will be prepared in manuscript.

WAR DIARY
or
INTELLIGENCE SUMMARY.
(*Erase heading not required.*)

Army Form C. 2118.

Hour, Date, Place	Summary of Events and Information	Remarks and references to Appendices
June 6th Billets in BETHUNE.	Voluntary church parade at 10-45 am.	
June 7th " "	Nos 2 & 3 Coys went to swimming baths. No 4 Coy went to hot water baths Ecole de Jeunes Filles. Trenches in CUINCHY section reconnoitred by officers of 2 & 4 Coy	
June 8th " "	Swimming baths again used by Nos 1, 2 & 4 Coys. More officers examined the trenches in the CUINCHY section. There are rumours that the enemy intend to use gas in this district. There was a tremendous thunderstorm about 1.30 pm. The G.O.C. 1st Div. went on leave to England.	The following N.C.O's & men of the Battn were awarded the D.C.M. 5885 Sgt Seymour C. 11430 Sgt Johnson G.W. 3360 Sgt Fascoigne H. 9020 Pte Rendall C. 11122 Pte Craig W.
June 9th	There was general swabbing by all Coys & the tobacco factory was thoroughly cleaned out. Coys went for a short route march in the evening. At abt 7.30 pm orders were received that 1st Brigade would relieve the 3rd Brigade in the CUINCHY section on the 10th inst. This Battn is to be in support in the CAMBRIN defences.	

(73989) W4141—463. 400,000. 9/14. H.&J.Ltd. Forms/C. 2118/10.

Army Form C. 2118.

Instructions regarding War Diaries and Intelligence Summaries are contained in F. S. Regs., Part II. and the Staff Manual respectively. Title pages will be prepared in manuscript.

WAR DIARY
or
INTELLIGENCE SUMMARY.
(Erase heading not required.)

Hour, Date, Place	Summary of Events and Information	Remarks and references to Appendices
June 10th Billets in BETHUNE.	The Battn paraded at 3.50pm & marched to various points round CAMBRIN – where Battn H.Q. were (to relieve 4th Bn Royal Welsh Fusiliers). After passing the cross Roads in BEUVRY platoons had to move with 100 yards between each platoon. There was a block in front & the Battn was not in it's new position until 8 pm. The Welsh Fusiliers had only on an average 100 men per coy so the Battn was rather crowded.	Lt. J. M. Younger } to hospital 2Lt. O. J. Style } sick.
June 11th CAMBRIN DEFENCES	The guns all round were extremely active. No 4 Coy in CUINCHY supporting point were rather heavily shelled by 5.9 guns but no casualties.	2Lt. O. J. Style from hospital Major A. J. E. Egerton went to hospital "sick"
June 12th	Our guns again active. The noise in CAMBRIN is incessant day & night.	2Lt. W. Johnston returned from leave. Other Ranks Killed. 1.
June 13th	At 5 pm Nos 1 & 4 Coys moved up to relieve the right & support coys of the Scots Guards in A.2. Nos 2 & 3 Coys moved up to relieve the centre & left coys at 5.30 pm. Relief completed by 7.30 pm without casualty	A draft of 28 N.C.O's & men joined the Battn at 8 pm. 2Lt. W. Johnston wounded at 12 mn.
June 14th Trenches nr CUINCHY A.2	A great deal of shelling by our own guns. Battn H.Qrs shelled by pip-squeaks but no damage done.	Capt Darell took over 2nd in command. Other Ranks wounded 1. missing 1.

(73989) W4141—463. 400,000. 9/14. H.&J.Ltd. Forms/C. 2118/10.

Instructions regarding War Diaries and Intelligence Summaries are contained in F. S. Regs., Part II. and the Staff Manual respectively. Title pages will be prepared in manuscript.

WAR DIARY
or
INTELLIGENCE SUMMARY.
(*Erase heading not required.*)

Army Form C. 2118.

Hour, Date, Place	Summary of Events and Information	Remarks and references to Appendices
June 15th. Trenches at CUINCHY	Again very heavy shelling all day. About 6 pm the Canadians & other Divisions north of the LA BASSÉE Canal attacked. From 5 to 6 pm our heavy howitzers shelled the brickstacks & the front trenches were cleared.	Lt J. C. Wynne Finch (No 3 Coy.) & Lt C. E. Tufnell (No 2 Coy) rejoined the Battn. Other ranks wounded 1.
June 16th. TRENCHES at CUINCHY	At 6.30 am orders were received that the Battn would be relieved by 2nd Brigade about 3.30 pm. The day was a fairly quiet one & the relief was carried out by 6 pm & on completion of relief the Bn marched back by coys to billets in Montmorency Barracks - BETHUNE. No 3 Coy was billeted in a house opposite the front gate. During the night of the 15th-16th the Germans tried to establish a sap or trench along their edge of a crater in front of No 1 Coy. They were dispersed by a bombing party but were able under cover of an early morning mist to complete their work. While the relief was being carried out another attack was launched just N. of the canal. The trenches taken the night before had been lost by bombing. Our guns were firing fast over our heads while the relief was being carried out, supporting this attack. The enemy shelled the junction of HARLEY ST. & LA BASSÉE road just as the relief was being completed but no damage was done.	Wounded. Other Ranks 6 (all wounded by 1 rifle grenade)

(73989) W4141—463. 400,000. 9/14. H.&J.Ltd. Forms/C. 2118/10.

Instructions regarding War Diaries and Intelligence Summaries are contained in F. S. Regs., Part II. and the Staff Manual respectively. Title pages will be prepared in manuscript.

WAR DIARY
or
INTELLIGENCE SUMMARY.
(Erase heading not required.)

Army Form C. 2118.

Hour, Date, Place	Summary of Events and Information	Remarks and references to Appendices
June 17th. Billets in MONTMORENCY BKS BETHUNE.	The Battn is at 2 hours notice. 50% of N.C.O's & men granted leave. Heavy firing at 8 pm in direction of FESTUBERT. At 11.30pm the Bn was put on 1 hrs notice.	2Lt. R.F. Pratt-Barlow joined the Battn (posted to No 3 Coy)
June 18th. " "	The Brigadier went on leave & Lt Col. J. Ponsonby took over command of the Brigade. Capt G. Darell took over command of Battn. Swimming & hot water baths allotted to the Bn.	
June 19th. " "	Many rumours about. The whole Div is withdrawn & the London Scottish & Black Watch are moved from BETHUNE to LAPUGNOY. The Battn was put on very short notice.	Major A.G. Egerton returned from Hospital. Lt. J. Wynne Finch to No 1 Coy to take command.
June 20th. " "	The Battn on 2 hrs notice again & was in waiting. Col. Sutton visited the Battn. Permission given for upkeep of Drums.	2Lt. N. P. Sutton went on leave to G.H.Q.
June 21st. "	Cpls had a "shouting" class.	
June 22nd. "	Orders received for working parties of near CAMBRIN at 12.30pm 7am of 425 men & 4 officers. Conference on bombing down German trenches.	Lt. Hon. T. Agar Robartes granted short leave to England.

(73989) W4141—463. 400,000. 9/14. H.&J.Ltd. Forms/C. 2118/10.

Army Form C. 2118.

Instructions regarding War Diaries and Intelligence Summaries are contained in F. S. Regs., Part II. and the Staff Manual respectively. Title pages will be prepared in manuscript.

WAR DIARY
or
INTELLIGENCE SUMMARY.
(*Erase heading not required.*)

Hour, Date, Place	Summary of Events and Information	Remarks and references to Appendices
June 23rd. Billets in BETHUNE. MONTMORENCY BKS.	A telegram was sent to the "Prince of Wales. H.Q. 1st Corps. From your ~~brother~~ fellow Guardsmen in the Coldstream, many congratulations". Corps class again assembled. Working parties again found. Orders received about 8.30pm that the Division would move into a new billeting area on the 24th inst. No move before 10 am.	
June 24th. Moved to billets in BURBURE	At 5.30 am orders were received that the Bn less the fatigue parties working under R.E. would move at 9.45 am to billets in ~~BEUV~~ BURBURE. abt 8 miles west. Arrived in BURBURE abt 12.45pm ~~tot~~ after a hot march. The men marched very badly. Their feet get in a very bad condition after trenches. The billets were not clear when we arrived so Battn halted & had dinners on the green. Eventually moving in about 3pm. The Bn took over from the 8th Black Watch. 9th Division. (the first of the new army. As only abt half the Bn came in all were able to get under cover.	

Instructions regarding War Diaries and Intelligence Summaries are contained in F. S. Regs., Part II. and the Staff Manual respectively. Title pages will be prepared in manuscript.

WAR DIARY
or
INTELLIGENCE SUMMARY.
(*Erase heading not required.*)

Army Form C. 2118.

Hour, Date, Place	Summary of Events and Information	Remarks and references to Appendices
June 25th Billets in BURBURE	Billets are very scarce & crowded. a wet day. The fatigue parties left behind in BETHUNE rejoined the Bn about 12. noon. Two men a day of those who had been out the whole time were allowed on leave for 8 days. T.F.O. Conference at 5.30 pm on bombing & march discipline by all officers & platoon commanders.	
June 26th " " "	The Bn went for a route march at 9am via LILLERS BOURBEC & ECQUEDECQUES. returning to billets abt 11.30 am. Marching much improved. about 6 pm news was received that the Division would return immediately to the trenches.	2nd Lt. N.C. P. Sutton leave to England.
June 27th " " "	At 9 am. Nos 1 & 2 Coys left billets to practise the attack in connection with Grenadiers (or bombers). Nos 3 & 4 practised the same thing during the afternoon. Lts Coyne Finch & Tufnell ordered to join the 2nd & 3rd Bns respectively. as they were two of the original subalterns of the Battn we offered to send two others instead. Orders received abt 9 pm that the Brigade would move at 2.30 pm next day. Lt. Col. C. E. Stewart C.M.G. took over command of the Brigade in temporary absence of Brig Gen. H. C. Lowther sick	Lt. Col. J. Ponsonby granted leave to England

Army Form C. 2118.

Instructions regarding War Diaries and Intelligence Summaries are contained in F. S. Regs., Part II. and the Staff Manual respectively. Title pages will be prepared in manuscript.

WAR DIARY
or
INTELLIGENCE SUMMARY.
(*Erase heading not required.*)

Hour, Date, Place	Summary of Events and Information	Remarks and references to Appendices
June 28th Billets in BURBURE	Orders received at 10am that the Brigade would not move – a wet day. No 3 Coy held a concert. 2/Lts Wynne Finch & Tufnell who had been ordered to join the 2nd & 3rd Bns respectively were kept & a proposal was put forward to send 2/Lts Riley & Peake instead. This was approved by the O.C. Bns but thrown out by the A-G. Orders for move received at 10pm.	2/Lts Hon E. K. Digby & 2/Lt Hon C. Noel returned from leave
June 29th Billets in BURBURE to " " VAUDRICOURT	The Bn moved off at 10.45am & marched well until within 1½ miles of their destination – when owing to an increase in the pace about 15 men fell out. The Bn arrived in billets abt 2.30pm. The billets were very crowded & not very clean. at 5pm. 2/Lts Wynne Finch & Tufnell proceeded to join 2nd & 3rd Bns	2/Lt R. M. Wright rejoined the Bn & took over command of the machine gunners.
June 30th Billets in VAUDRICOURT.	Instruction of corporals & bombers was continued but interfered with by rain. Billets cleaned up.	2/Lts R. T. Philipson & F. M. Fisher joined Bn & posted to Nos 4 & 1 Coys respectively

(73989) W4141—463. 400,000. 9/14. H.&J.Ltd. Forms/C. 2118/10.

A P P E N D I C E S .

"A" Form. Army Form C. 2121.

MESSAGES AND SIGNALS.

No. of Message..........

Prefix.......Code.......m. Office of Origin and Service Instructions	Words / Charge — Sent At.......m. To....... By.......	This message is on a/c of: ....Service. (Signature of "Franking Officer.")	Recd. at.......m. Date....... From....... By.......

TO — The Private Secretary

Sender's Number	Day of Month	In reply to Number	AAA
*			

The	three	Battalion	Coldstream	Guards
in	France	~~send~~	~~many~~	~~to the~~
~~congratulations~~		wish	your	Majesty
many	congratulations	today		

From

Place

Time

The above may be forwarded as now corrected. (Z)

Censor — Signature of Addressor or person authorised to telegraph in his name.

* This line should be erased if not required.

Printed and supplied by Gale & Polden Ltd., Aldershot, in blocks of 50, 9d. per block, to fit the "Handy Refill Case."

"C" Form (Duplicate). Army Form C. 2123.

MESSAGES AND SIGNALS. No. of Message

Charges to Pay. £ s. d.

Office Stamp.

Service Instructions. General Headqrs

Handed in at Office 12-15 m. Received 1-9 m.

TO 1st Bn Coldstm Gds

Sender's Number	Day of Month	In reply to Number	AAA
F 2332	3rd June		

Following from the King "The Message which I have received from the Three Battalions of My Coldstream Guards at the front on the anniversary of my Birthday has greatly touched me aaa please convey to all ranks my warmest thanks for their congratulations and good wishes and tell them how proud I am of their achievements"

FROM Military Secretary

PLACE & TIME

Wt. W. 9668—1672. 50,000 Pads. 1584—1/15. S. B. Ltd.—Forms/C.2123.

. . . .

In the event of BETHUNE being heavily shelled, the four Battalions billeted in BETHUNE will be moved by order of the Brigadier to the following places, where they will remain with companies dispersed as far as possible, and under cover from Aeroplane observation.

Scots Guards to the wood (not marked on map) at E.22.b.8.5 Route. E.16.a - road junction E.22.a.6.5 - E.22.b.~~6~~ 1.1 - thence by track running north-east to the wood.

Brigade Headquarters and Coldstream Guards to the grounds immediately West of PRIEURE ST PRY, E.22.a.5.5.

Black Watch to the enclosure immediately south of PRIEURE ST PRY, E.22.c.1.9.

London Scottish along the Avenue and on west side of PRIEURE ST PRY E.21.b.9.5.

~~[struck out]~~ ROUTE. RUE DE LILLE - BOULEVARD THIERS - road junction E.16.c - road junction E.21.b.

In the event of BEUVRY being heavily shelled, the Camerons will move at once under orders of O.C. to covered position about F.7.d and will send an orderly to the Railway bridge at E. 18.b.7.5 to direct orderlies who may be sent from Brigade Headquarters.

The following transport only will be taken, remainder remaining in their present billets :-

Machine Gun limbers.
Water Carts.
Maltese Carts.

The Coldstream Guards and Camerons will each take 3 S.A.A. Carts in addition.

[signature]

Major,

4/8/15. Brigade Major, 1st Guards Brigade.

S E C R E T.

C.O.1.Gds. . . . .

Secret information has been received that pressure pump used for asphyxiating gas has been sent to ILLIES. The men working them have been issued with helmets.

The Major-General is sure that ~~this his~~ if the instructions already issued are carried out and sharp look-out kept, troops have nothing to fear from gas.

Sharp look out both by day and by night is absolutely essential, good ears are as necessary as good eyes, as the hissing noise of the gas being liberated can often be heard before the gas itself can be seen.

The smoke helmets which will be taken over as Trench Stores on relieving other Battalions in the trenches must in the first instance be issued to troops holding the front line.

[signature]

Major,

8/6/15. Brigade Major, 1st Guards Brigade.

"A" Form.

Army Form C. 2121.

MESSAGES AND SIGNALS.

No. of Message

Prefix .... Code .... m. | Words | Charge

Office of Origin and Service Instructions.

Sent
At .... m.
To
By

This message is on a/c of: .... Service.

(Signature of "Franking Officer.")

Recd. at .... m.
Date
From
By

TO Coldstream Guards

Sender's Number	Day of Month	In reply to Number	AAA
* Z A 21	16th.		

1st Division advise us as follows, begins :- "1st Army report at 5-45 pm that French attack has captured front line of German trenches along nearly all the front and has progressed further in many parts AAA Observers report having seen French infantry on crest of ridge S.E. of Souchez." Ends.

Received from 1st Division later, at 7-30 p.m. "Following from 1st Corps Begins reports received 5-45 pm show that 8th Liverpools have occupied German trenches at L 10 and Scots Fusiliers at I 2 - I 4 AAA Ends."

From 1st Brigade.
Place
Time

The above may be forwarded as now corrected. (Z) [signature] Major.

Censor. Signature of Addressor or person authorised to telegraph in his name.

* This line should be erased if not required.

:02146—W. & S. Ltd., London.—W 14142/641—90,000—4/15. Forms C 2121/10.

Coldstream Guards
****

The following received from 1st Division, begins :-

"1st Army report begins Early in the night that portion of the 7th DIVISION between I 3 and I 4 was attacked by the Germans and driven back to our own lines AAA Subsequently the Canadians about H2-H5 were forced to withdraw AAA At 5 am. 51st DIVN reported that their right had been bombed out of K 6 and K 2 and had withdrawn to our own lines AAA Similarly left of 7th DIVN at J11-J13 were bombed out AAA These left Grenadiers at J10 with both flanks exposed and they also were forced back AAA About 5 am report received from 51st Divn that troops which had captured L9 and L10 were unable to retain points captured and were withdrawing then to original line AAA Germans in considerable strength AAA 2nd Army report that enemy's trenches N.W. from HOOGE Chateau to YPRES-ROULERS railway had been penetrated at various points AAA Further telegram from 1st Army states that 2nd Army have made further progress and have taken one hundred and eleven prisoners AAA"

1st Brigade. Major,

16th June 1915. Brigade Major, 1st Guards Brigade.

"A" Form.

MESSAGES AND SIGNALS.

Prefix............Code............m. | Words | Charge | *This message is on a/c of:* ....Service. | Date | From | By

Office of Origin and Service Instructions.

Sent — At..........m. To.......... By..........

(Signature of "Franking Officer.")

TO Coldstream Gds

Sender's Number	Day of Month	In reply to Number	AAA
* IA. 3.	24th		

Your fatigue party which is working under R.E. today near CAMBRIN can remain in its billets at BETHUNE tonight, and reform the battalion at BURBURE tomorrow AAA No further fatigue parties will be required after today by R.E.

From First Bde

Place

Time 5.30 am

The above may be forwarded as now corrected. (Z) [illegible]

Censor. Signature of Addressor or person authorised to telegraph in his name.

* This line should be erased if not required.

102146—W. & S. Ltd., London.—W 14142/641—90,000—4/15. Forms C 2121/10.

"A" Form.

Army Form C. 2121.

MESSAGES AND SIGNALS.

No. of Message ....

Prefix .... Code .... m. | Words | Charge

Office of Origin and Service Instructions.

Sent
At .... m.
To ....
By ....

This message is on a/c of: .... Service.

(Signature of "Franking Officer.")

Recd. at .... m.
Date
From
By

ARMY ZA 24 VI. 15 ZA TELEGRAPHS

TO Coldstream Gds
~~Scots Gds~~
~~Black Watch~~

Sender's Number	Day of Month	In reply to Number	AAA
* ZA. 2.	24th		

Reference Sheet 36 B 1.40.000

1. The Brigade will march as follows to billets in the area BURBURE – RAIMBERT.

Headquarters at ~~10~~ 9.15 am via ~~Fouquereuil~~ ANNEZIN – LABEUVRIERE – ALLOUAGNE to BURBURE.

Coldstream Gds at ~~10~~ 9.15 am via ANNEZIN – LABEUVRIERE thence by shortest route to BURBURE.

Black Watch at 10 am and London Scottish at 10.30 am via MARLES – LES – MINES – AUCHEL and RAIMBERT. Guides will meet these battalions at road junction C. 15 A. to direct them to their billets.

Scots Guards at 10 am and Camerons at 10.20 am via road north of the railway – LOZINGHEM to BURBURE.

2. Billeting parties will meet the Staff captain at ~~9.30~~ 8.45 am at BURBURE Church.

From First Bde

Place

Time 5.30 am.

The above may be forwarded as now corrected.

(Z) [signature]

Censor. Signature of Addressor or person authorised to telegraph in his name.

* This line should be erased if not required.

:02146--W. & S. Ltd., London.—W 14142/641—90,000—4/15. Forms C 2121/10.

"A" Form. Army Form C. 2121.

MESSAGES AND SIGNALS. No. of Message

Prefix ..... Code ..... m.	Words	Charge	This message is on a/c of:	Recd. at ..... m.
Office of Origin and Service Instructions.	Sent		..... Service.	Date
SECRET.	At ..... m.			From
	To			
	By		(Signature of "Franking Officer.")	By

TO Coll Gds

Sender's Number	Day of Month	In reply to Number	AAA
* 2 A 11	26th		

(1). First Brigade will not move before the 28th, probably not til before the 29th

(2). 1st Army is being re-organised as follows :-

Indian Corps. (51st, Lahore, Meerut Divns)
1st Corps. (2nd, 7th, 9th Divisions).
4th Corps. (1st, 47th, 48th Divisions).

(3). 4th Corps is taking over Sections, W.X.Y.&.Z.

(4). 1st Division is taking over the line from VERMELLES - LOOS Road exclusive, to the L of LES BRIQUES Road exclusive, 3rd Brigade on the right, 2nd Brigade on the left.

From 1st Brigade.

Place

Time 9.50 p.m.

Major, Brigade Major.

The above may be forwarded as now corrected. (Z)

Censor. Signature of Addressor or person authorised to telegraph in his name.

* This line should be erased if not required.

202146—W. & S. Ltd., London.—W 14142/611—20,000—4/15. Forms C 2121/10.

1st Infantry Brigade.

1st Division.

WAR DIARY

1st COLDSTREAM GUARDS.

J U L Y

1 9 1 5

Appendices.

On His Majesty's Service.

Instructions regarding War Diaries and Intelligence Summaries are contained in F. S. Regs., Part II. and the Staff Manual respectively. Title pages will be prepared in manuscript.

WAR DIARY
or
INTELLIGENCE SUMMARY.
(Erase heading not required.)

Army Form C. 2118.

Hour, Date, Place	Summary of Events and Information	Remarks and references to Appendices
July 1st Billets in VAUDRICOURT.	Coy practised the attack & bombing beginning with [illegible] Coy at 9 am. The trenches were rather too shallow & not on a wide enough front to make the practice a really good one. Brig. Gen. Feilding who had taken over command of 4th Bgde vice Ld Cavan promoted to Northumberland Division came to lunch.	Lt & Qr Mr Boyd went on short leave to England. Lt Hon. T. Agar Robartes returned from leave.
July 2nd	Cpls & Lance Sgts had a shouting class. Training of bombers continued. The remainder of the Bn improved the trenches for the practise of the attack.	
July 3rd	A very hot day. Training of Cpls & bombers continued. Battn Sports held in the afternoon. The Black Watch lent their band & Major Gen Haking C.B. gave away the prizes. Tug of war won by No 2 Coy. Sgt Searles won most of the running races. There was also a bombers race. Pte Longstaff won the old soldiers race with 33 years service (1 yard start per year).	
July 4th	The Battn practised the attack again with bombers – 2 coys at 8 am 2 coys at 9 am. Voluntary Church of England service at 11am.	Lt R. P. B. Sutton returned from short leave.

(73989) W4141—463. 400,000. 9/14. H.&J.Ltd. Forms/C. 2118/10.

Army Form C. 2118.

WAR DIARY
or
INTELLIGENCE SUMMARY

Hour, Date, Place.	Summary of Events and Information.	Remarks and ~~references~~ to Appendices
July 5th Billets in VAUDRICOURT to " " LABOURSE.	Owing to the open country the Battn had to move by platoons. No 2 Coy started at 12 noon + the whole Bn were not in new billets till 2.30 pm. The billets were not very clean. at 9.45 pm the Bn had to furnish a working party of 600 men to work on 2nd line trenches at VERMELLES. not much work was done as work had to be stopped at 1 am. The whole party was not back till 2.30 am.	Capt Darell granted leave to England.
July 6th Billets in LABOURSE.	Working party as on 5th again furnished. a party of 35 N.C.O's + men under Lt. R. Peake detailed to work with 23rd Field Coy R.E on dug outs until further orders.	Lt. Col J. Ponsonby returned from leave + took over command of the Brigade.

Army Form C. 2118.

WAR DIARY
or
INTELLIGENCE SUMMARY

Hour, Date, Place.		Summary of Events and Information.	Remarks and ~~references~~ to Appendices.
7-7-15.	LA BOURSE.	Bn digging all night	
8. 7. 15		Bn diggin all night	
9-7-15.	LA BOURSE	In the morning No 2 & 3 Coys. did a practice attack with bombers at the bombing ground at VAUDRICOURT. The Battalion relieved the Scots Guards in Y1 Section of trenches. Relief completed 1.30 A.M. 9th/10th.	A draft of 1 Sgt. 1 lance cpl and 23 men joined the Batt from the Base
10-7-15.	Trenches at LE RUTOIRE	Quiet day. Very little shelling. 11732 Pte Pope J. accidentally wounded by a bomb.	11732 Pte Pope J. accidentally wounded by a bomb
11-7-15.	" " "	Very quiet. Brig. General Lowther went round the trenches in the early morning.	
12-7-15		Very quiet. 7 O.R. went on leave this morning. Fine but windy.	
13. 7. 15	" " "	The Bn was relieved by the Scots Gds	
13. 7. 15	Billets in VERMELLES	The Bn was digging all night	

Army Form C. 2118.

WAR DIARY
or
INTELLIGENCE SUMMARY

Hour, Date, Place.	Summary of Events and Information.	Remarks and ~~references~~ to Appendices.
July 15th. Billets in VERMELLES	Coy commanders went round 2nd & 3rd line trenches in two parties one in the morning at 7am under the Col & the other at 2pm under the 2nd in command. Sir Henry Rawlinson visited Bn. H.Q. – Working parties out all night.	Lt & adj ~~M.~~ B. Smith returned from leave. Lt. C. J. Riley proceeded on leave.
July 16th. Billets in VERMELLES to trenches in LE RUTOIRE	Coy Commanders continued their tour of inspection. Nos 4 & 3 Coys left at 2.30 & 2.45 pm respectively to relieve Scots Gds in Y.1. Nos 2 & 1 Coys left about 4.30pm. The whole relief completed about 6.30pm.	
July 17th. Trenches E of VERMELLES (LE RUTOIRE)	A very quiet day. A lot of work was done during night on new front trench – not yet completed & only held by groups during the day.	
July 18th. " "	About 7 pm a Zeppelin was seen some little distance to the South – going west.	

Army Form C. 2118.

WAR DIARY
or
INTELLIGENCE SUMMARY

Hour, Date, Place.	Summary of Events and Information.	Remarks and references to Appendices.
July 19th. Trenches E of VERMELLES (LE RUTOIRE)	another very quiet day. about 4 pm the Corps Commander (Sir Henry Rawlinson) came round the trenches. & had tea at Bn. H.Q.	
to billets in BETHUNE	at 9.30 pm the relief of the Bn. by 1st Northants was begun. The whole Bn. was out of the trenches by 11.30 pm but was not all in billets in BETHUNE till 2.30 am.	
July 20th. Billets in BETHUNE	Battalion resting after 14 nights successive digging fatigues (each every night) a few shells fell just short of Bn. Billetting area	
July 21st " "	Range near LABEUVRIERE allotted to corps. The 2nd & 3rd Bns. came into billets in BETHUNE News of the formation of a Guards Division confirmed & that a Pioneer Bn. to the Division is to be formed from the 4th Bn.	
July 22nd " "	Bombing ground at BOIS des MONTAGNES allotted to bombers of corps. at a trench mortar course held at VERQUIN	

Army Form C. 2118.

WAR DIARY
or
INTELLIGENCE SUMMARY

Hour, Date, Place.	Summary of Events and Information.	Remarks and references to Appendices.
July 22nd. Billets in BETHUNE.	in the afternoon an accident occurred in which 1 officer (Lt Mitchell) & 2 men of the BLACK WATCH were killed & 4 men of this Bn wounded. BETHUNE was also heavily shelled in the afternoon & there were many casualties in the ÉCOLE de Jeunes Filles. 1 man of 1st Bn wounded –	2nd Lt. F.R. was accidentally wounded by a bomb in the morning –
July 23rd " " "	Range near CANNEZIN allotted to coys in the morning.	
July 2	an Inter Regimental boxing competition was started on the sports ground under the management of Major Egerton & Captain Bentinck.	
July 24th " " "	The inter Regimental boxing finished. The 1st Bn won the light heavies (Sgt Gibson) & heavy weights (Pte Ransome). There was also a horse show for the 1st Bgde. The Bn won both the officers jumping (Lt A. B. Smith on Lt G. A. Campbells mare which had been out in France all the war) & the mens (Dr. Sgt Kidd on a transport horse) The best charger was also won by 1st Bn & the prize for the best horse that had been out all the war.	

Army Form C. 2118.

WAR DIARY
or
INTELLIGENCE SUMMARY

Hour, Date, Place.	Summary of Events and Information.	Remarks and references to Appendices.
July 25th Billets in BETHANE to " " SAILLY LABOURSE	at 1 pm the Bn. started to move by platoons at 200 yds interval to SAILLY LABOURSE. The move was completed by 3.30 pm. The billets were taken over in a moderate state from the 2nd Welsh Regiment. No 2 Coy had to dig just E of VERMELLES during the night on HULLUCH ALLEY C.T.	
July 26th " " "	Three Coys worked by day } on the VERMELLES One Coy " " night } portion of the GRENAY Line all ~~officers~~ coy commanders went up to Z.2 section.	1 man killed with the Brigade wiring party.
July 27th " " "	Same digging fatigues as before.	2 Lt. C. E. Green rejoined the Bn (morning) Lt. Hon. M. D. H. Browne " " (afternoon) Capt E. B. Gregge Hopwood joined " "
July 28th " " to trenches S of the La BASSÉE BETHUNE road.	The Bn. relieved the Scots Gds in the trenches & left billets by coys starting at 3.30 pm.	

Army Form C. 2118.

WAR DIARY
or
INTELLIGENCE SUMMARY

Hour, Date, Place.	Summary of Events and Information.	Remarks and references to Appendices.
July 28th cont. Trenches S of BETHUNE – LA BASSEE Road.	The relief of the Scots Guards was completed by 6.15pm. Enemy dropped a few shells into CAMBRIN just after our last coy had passed through. They also dropped a few shells into CAILLY after we had left it. The trenches the Bn went into (Z2) were held by 3 coys in the front line (No 1 on the left, 2 in the centre 4 on the right) & No 3 Coy in support. Z2 is probably one of the worst sections of the line – the trenches just S. of LA BASSEE road being especially bad. The Germans were nowhere further away than 200 yds & in some places only 15. There were 3 mine craters in front of this part of the line. The Germans bomb trench mortar & send over rifle grenades continuously. They had been allowed to get v. much out of hand. During the night 2Lt. C.R. Green (bomb officer) & Lt. Hon T. Agar Robartes organised a bombing party & silenced the German bombers opposite our centre in Etna crater.	1 O.R. killed. 2 O.R. wounded. [2 Sgts (Sgt Hatton & Sgt Jackson D.C.M. [illegible]) were hit about 7.30 pm by rifle grenade. Sgt Hatton died in about quarter of an hour & Jackson subsequently died of his wounds.]
July 29th " " "	Sir Henry Rawlinson & the brigadier came round the trenches at 6am. The enemy shelled our trenches v. heavily from 7am to 2pm. A fairly quiet night.	1. O.R. killed. 7 O.R. wounded.

Instructions regarding War Diaries and Intelligence Summaries are contained in F. S. Regs., Part II. and the Staff Manual respectively. Title pages will be prepared in manuscript.

WAR DIARY
or
INTELLIGENCE SUMMARY.
(*Erase heading not required.*)

Army Form C. 2118.

Hour, Date, Place	Summary of Events and Information	Remarks and references to Appendices
July 30th Trenches S. of LA BASSEE Road	If anything there was a little less bombing & trench mortaring on the part of the enemy. Some of our own shells seemed to fall rather short. The gunners were notified & subsequently there was a good deal of correspondence on the subject — about which there can have really been no doubt. Two German working parties were discovered during the night just S. of LA BASSEE Rd. One was dispersed by bombing — the other by artillery fire.	1. O.R. killed. 9 O.R. wounded.
July 31st " " " " to Billets in SAILLY LABOURSE	Enemy's guns far less active & bombs & grenades somewhat less numerous. The Bn was relieved commencing at 2 pm by the Scots Gds. The relief was completed & the Bn back in billets by 5.30 pm.	1. O.R. killed 2 O.R. wounded.

(73989) W4141—463. 400,000. 9/14. H.&J.Ltd. Forms/C. 2118/10.

Reference:
BETHUNE MAP
Sheets combined
1/40000

Orders for relief on
night of 19th–20th by H. C. J. Ponsonby
C.M.G. D.S.O

1. The Battn: will be relieved on the night of 19th–20th about 10 pm by the 1st Northants.

2. One guide per platoon will report to the drill Sgt at Bn. H.Q at 9 pm.

3. The billeting party under 2Lt J. R. Woods will be at the H.Q of 9th Liverpools in FAUBOURG D'ARRAS, BETHUNE at 12 noon.

4. All trench stores including S.A.A & bombs will be handed over & a receipt obtained. (N.B Periscopes are not trench stores). (a list of Trench Stores handed over to be sent to the OR by 9 am.)

5. all picks & shovels will be returned to Bn. H.Q by 7am. 10 picks & 10 shovels may be kept by each coy for use during the day but these must be brought to Bn. H.Q & handed to the pioneer Sgt by 8 pm.

6. On completion of relief coys will march independently to billets in FAUBOURG D'ARRAS BETHUNE, via L.4.C.10.4. & SAILLY LABOURSE.
Coys will be formed up as coys before leaving VERMELLES.

7. The wiring parties will rejoin coys as they leave the trenches.

TO

Sender's Number.	Day of Month	In reply to Number	AAA
*			

8 The Battn will be at 4 hours notice while in BETHUNE

9. No 2 Coy will be in waiting from 8 pm 19.9.15 to 8 pm 20.9.15

10. Bgde H.Q will be at FOUQUIERES E 20.b.5.5

11. Officers mess stores must be at Bn H.Q by 9.30 pm.

12. Officers chargers will be at the Church in VERMELLES.

[signature] 1st C.G.

From

Place

Time

The above may be forwarded as now corrected.

Censor.

(Z)

Signature of Addressor or person authorised to telegraph in his name.

* This line should be erased if not required.

(688-9) —McC. & Co. Ltd., London.— W 14142/641. 225,000 4/15. Forms C 2121/10.

APPENDICES.

4th Corps No.378 (G).

1st Division.

The following information has been received regarding the use of asphyziating gas shells by the Germans in their attack on the cemetry at SOUCHEZ on the night of the 11th/12th instant -

(a). Large numbers of ths shells were fired on the French trenches, batteries and observation posts.

(b). The gas given off by shells had a somewhat pleasant aromatic small. It first effected the eyes, causing them to water copiously. Goggles were found sufficient protection provided they fitted tightly to the face.

(Sgd) P.Game, Major, forBBrig Genl.
G.S. IVth Corps.

(2).

Coldstream Guards

Forwarded for your information.

The Major-General directs that as soon as the aromatic smell is noticed, all troops in the vicinity will be ordered to put on their respiratotors.

R G Graham Captain,

17th July 1915. for Brigade Major, 1st Guards Brigad

SECRET.

Milli Gr................

The attached copy of Notes by the Major-General and Memorandum on "Village Fighting" is forwarded for your information.

[signature] Captain,

15/7/15. for Brigade Major, 1st Guards Brigade.

1st Div.No.S/34/G.

Head Quarters,

IVth Corps.

With reference to your H.R.S. 261,dated 10th.inst.,I think the report is a most useful one and contains many valuable suggestions. Our only experience of village fighting in 1st Division was the attack in GIVENCHY on 21st December, and the counter stroke against the Germans at the same place on 25th January,one carried out by the 1st Guards Brigade,and the other by 3rd Brigade. On each of these occasions the Germans had not had time to establish themselves in the village and were driven out with great loss by the bayonet. Neither side used bombs,and the fighting inside houses,which went on some time after the village had been cleared,was done with the bayonet.

Paras.3 and 11 of the report,indicate the great importance of discovering which houses the enemy have specially prepared for defence. The French Artillery without this knowledge were unable to deal with these houses,whereas the German Artillery,believing them to be captured by the French,and knowing their importance and exact locality,were able to blow them to pieces.

The great importance of good Grenadiers is clearly brought out,and it is probable that for this class of fighting ,the Grenadiers and grenade carriers should be armed with bombs and a loaded stick,and not carry a rifle.

The value of trench mortars of a light pattern which can easily be carried forward is shown,and I do not think we have sufficient of these weopons or sufficient men trained in their use. The mortars we have are constantly being used in the trenches,but I am slowly drawing out detatchments to put them through a course of instruction outside the trenches. I cannot do very much however,until we get mortars. The 2" are excellent for trench work and also the 1½",but they are both heavy for attack purposes.

Petrol tins should be available for carrying up water, one man carrying two with a strap over his shoulder. This is the best method I have heard of yet,and one which we always employ in our trenches.

The very best troops are required for village fighting so as to ensure a constant pressure forward,otherwise the attack stops,and the men in front block the way,and it is then useless to send up more troops on the top of them.

A time will doubtless come when further progress cannot be made, and it will be necessary to revert to mining or to sapping. It is ~~desirable~~ desirable, therefore, that a mining company should be at hand with all necessary mining tools, and light timber for linings. One or more Field Cos, R.E. should be available according to the size of the village, provided with the following tools, and infantry carrying parties to take them up :-

(i). Saphead shields, possibly on wheels.

(ii). Sandbags, loophole plates, picks, crowbars & explosives.

The organisation of parties to take forward large quantities of hand grenades, rifle grenades, trench mortar ammunition and S.A.A. together with asphyxiating grenades and mountain guns, would also be most useful.

The defence of villages also requires careful attention, especially as regards wiring up the inside of the village so as to direct the tide of attack straight into the KEEPS, where it will come under heavy machine gun, artillery and rifle and grenade fire from the defences.

Both GIVENCHY and NEUVE CHAPELLE were prepared in this way be the Division and VERMELLES is now being similarly prepared.

13/7/15. (Sgd) R.Haking Major-General,

VILLAGE FIGHTING.

The following notes have been compiled from reports received from the French concerning their attacks round ARRAS.

1. Village fighting has proved so difficult and so costly to the assailant that the French are determined not to undertake an attack on a village unless it is absolutely unavoidable.

They consider it preferable to pass by the village, dealing with it later by means of heavy artillery, and trusting to lack of supplies of all sorts to bring about its downfall.

2. At the same time, such a course may not be possible because the village may be so placed that the enemy holding it may be able to prevent guns being brought up to support the troops in front, or supplies and reinforcements being sent forward to them.

In this case the capture of the village may be essential.

An attempt to capture a village by "coup de main" will probably be very costly. Continuous efforts at progress day and night, based on a well thought out plan, appear to offer the best and cheapest method of success.

3. An attack must not be undertaken without a thorough artillery preparation, which should be made by the heaviest artillery, and last several days.

This prolonged bombardment may not cause much actual damage to the hostile personnel, for the dug-outs and cellars in which the Germans live are proof against practically everything. It does, however, shake the morale of the defenders and damage his machine-gun emplacements; moreover, the continual shifting of bricks and masonry restricts, or at least alters, their field of fire, and has in some cases trapped whole detachments in their dug-outs.

4. Both **CARENCY** and **ABLAIN ST NAZAIRE** were practically surrounded before they fell, the French approaching by saps and digging round them, or occupying houses which had been previously destroyed by artillery. **NEUVILLE** was taken house by house.

5. The first difficulty met with was to secure a footing or "bite" in the village. Once this was accomplished the morale of the attackers and their fighting power immediately increased.

6. When the men penetrated into the village, the bulk of the houses had already been destroyed, so that fighting was from one heap of stones to another, and down the street. Barricades were a feature of the fighting, and these had to be turned. Occasionally there were short rushes in the open across the fields, but these were rare after the first charge up to the vicinity of the villages.

7. Machine guns were the main weapon of the German defence, but the French also used them in the attack with considerable effect.

(a). The German machine guns were generally placed in cellars where they had a narrow and short field of fire; when this front was reduced by the displacement of stones as a result of the bombardment, grenadiers were able to approach behind the fallen masonry, and "lob" grenades into the cellars. This proved very effective. The German machine guns were also sometimes placed in the roofs of such houses as were left standing; from here they were used to search communication trenches, sweep streets, protect flanks, or command barricades.

(b).

(b). The French in the attack used them to cover the flanks of their attacks, which were unavoidably delivered from a narrow front; they also them to search those places where the enemy's machine guns were supposed to be, and they claim that this method was effective. In an advance the machine guns followed the attacking troops as closely as possible, and were always pushed into the most advanced point gained, from which it was gradually found possible to enfilade, or take in reverse, some point of the enemy's line.

8. Trench mortars are reported to have been the most effective weapon in village fighting. It is stated that NEUVILLE would not have been taken but for the French trench mortars.

The capture of this village can be divided into stages, each stage being limited by the raneg and sphere of action of the trench mortars available.

Both large and small mortars were used. The largest bomb thrown was one from a 58 cm mortar firing an aerial torpedo; at one stage of the attack on NEUVILLE there was a pause of 4 days until these mortars could be brought up. Both here and at CARENCY, mountain guns were used effectively also.

9. In addition to their rifles and bayonets, the infantry carried knives and hand grenades, but the supply of the latter was seriously interfered with by the hostile "tir de barrage" which was directed principally on the damaged communication trenches. It was calculated that only 1 grenade in 4 of those sent up from the rear ever reached the troops.

No special demand appears to have existed for tools such as axes, crowbars, etc, nor for explosives. The reason for this appears to lie in the fact that above ground houses were mainly destroyed, while in the cellars the defenders were driven out by high explosive grenades, or asphyxiated by gas bombs.

These bombs were largely used for this purpose, and also for destroying small parties who were surrounded in their bomb proofs and who refused to surrender.

10. Body shields were not used possibly because they were not available. Steel caps were sometimes used; the Medical Officers reported favourably on them, and the moral effect on the wearer was reported to be good.

Many men, however, threw them away because

(a). They found them heavy.

(b). They considered that wounds were made more dangerous by their use.

11. Heavy artillery was found very effective when it could be employed, but once the attackers penetrated the village, the guns were compelled, for fear of damaging their own infantry, to restrict themselves to forming "barrages" behind the enemy's line.

This curtailmdnt of artillery support was unfortunate as in several cases strong "points d'appui" in the middle of the villages were able to hold up the attackers for considerable periods of time.

At NEUVILLE some of these strongly fortified houses held out after the rest of rhe village had been taken; these were only reduced by the German artillery who thought they had been captured by the French, and knowing their importance blew them to pieces.

12.

12. There does not appear to have been any method used for communicating between the infantry and the artillery which we have not already tried. The telephone lines were constantly out and there was too much dust and smoke to see visual signals or even daylight fireworks.

The whole of the artillery work was done according to pre-arranged orders.

13. During the attack on CARENCY, the attacking troops were not relieved for three nights, although the fighting was severe.

The French distribute their men on a very narrow front, i.e., a regiment fought of the front of a platoon. By this method they ckaim that they can constantly ~~relieve~~ relieve their men in the front line without having a change ~~of~~ in command. The troops when they are relieved sleep where they are in the captured cellars or dug-outs, and the relieving troops continue to attack uninterruptedly.

As stated in para ~~6~~ 9, the hostile "tir de barrage" made an actual relief by a large body of fresh troops a very costly affair, moreover, so closely were the combatants engaged, that attempts to withdraw men for relief in any numbers invariably ~~mun~~ meant loss of ground. The scattered nature of the fighting, and the fact that the position of the front troops was known only to a few of the subordinate leaders on the spot, made any attempts at relief on a large scale and on a preconceived plan an impossibility.

14. For the same reason, the supply of food and water presents serious difficulties.

At NEUVILLE the French found food and water which had been left by the Germans, and were so saved a great deal of anxiety. The only solution seems to be for the men to carry the maximum amount of reserve rations and full waterbottles.

The men detailed for the attack carried bread, sugar, coffee, and cold meat for the current day, and two days reserve rations.

Water was taken to selected spots under Divisional arrangements at night. Hot meals were similarly brought up.

250 rounds of S.A.A. per man was carried.

15. The experience of the French went to show the necessity of having specially selected fatigue parties under good officers for the purpose of bringing up anything that was wanted in front.

The work was done at first by Territorials, but they were found insufficient, and whole comp nies of regular infantry and detachments detailed specially for the purpose were used in addition.

16. Another problem was the evacuation of the wounded. They were treated in the first instance in the captured positions, and evacuated by night by special communication trenches.

Prisoners were similarly dealt with.

IVth Corps No.738 (G).

Concealment of movements of Troops and Traffic towards the Front.

Owing to the open country eastwards it is necessary for special precautions to be taken in regard to the movement of troops and traffic towards the front.

1. It is essential that motor-cars, lorries, and horses should not be placed in a position near any Divisional or Brigade Headquarters from which they can be seen from the front.

2. (a). Except at night or when especially ordered, troops must not use any roads east of the line F.21.central - F.26.b.5.0 - E.24.central - E.28.c.10.0 - K.4.a.10.5 - VAUDRICOURT - HOUCHIN - BARLIN road in larger numbers than a platoon at a time, and a distance of 400 - 800 yards should be observed between platoons. No more than two wagons, or more than 4 horses or men on horseback, are to use roads east of this line at the same time except at intervals of 400 - 800 yards. No lorries are allowed east of SAILLY - LABOURSE barricade without a pass from an A.P.M.

(b). All roads east of SAILLY-LABOURSE between the SAILLY - LABOURSE - LENS road and the BETHUNE - LA BASSEE road are closed by day, except the road running S.W. from VERMELLES and joining the main road at L.18.c, which may be used as in (a) above.

(c). The area SAILLY LABOURSE - LABOURSE (L.2.central) - NOEUX LES MINES Station - Square L.16.d - NOYELLES LES VERMELLES is not to be used by day except in exceptional circumstances.

3. By night, motor vehicles using any road east of the line mentioned in 2 (a) above are not to carry lighted head lamps. Troops and vehicles marching are not to show lights except in an emergency.

4. Officers proceeding forward of the line mentioned above in motor-cars must endeavour in daytime to use roads other than those running at right angles to the enemy's front, & must avoid raising dust.

5. For the purpose of training, the troops billeted in NOEUX LES MINES may route march in the area west of that town under such arrangements as the Brigade Commander concerned deems advisable, having due regard to the safety of the troops and the necessity of not drawing hostile attention to the area.

6. The traffic of motor-cars, motor ambulances, and motor-cyclists from NOEUX LES MINES to MAZINGARBE, and vice versa, is to be reduced to a minimum. Motor vehicles must endeavour to use, by day, roads other than the direct road.

7. The use of the new road in MAZINGARBE running on the east side of the line of villas between the chateau and LE SAULCHOY Farm is forbidden for all except necessary traffic.

8. Whenever possible, arrangements should be made for exercising horses off the roads. If it is necessary to use roads, the exercising should be done in the early morning, and in no case is one man to be in charge of more than two horses. Exercising of ~~horse~~ horses east of the line mentioned in 2 (a) above is forbidden except in the case of units billeted or bivouacking to the east of that road. Special care is to be taken that horses of these units are exercised in places where they are not exposed to hostile view and fire.

= = = = = = = = = = = = = = = = =

www.ingramcontent.com/pod-product-compliance
Lightning Source LLC
Chambersburg PA
CBHW081426160426
43193CB00013B/2203
* 9 7 8 1 4 7 4 5 0 2 5 5 9 *